AF584974

Be Bold

Be Bold

Alexis Fernandez-Preiksa

First published in Australia in 2021 by Affirm Press,
a Simon & Schuster (Australia) Pty Limited company
This edition published in 2026
Bunurong/Boon Wurrung Country
28 Thistlethwaite Street, South Melbourne VIC 3205

Affirm Press is located on the unceded land of the Bunurong/Boon Wurrung peoples of the Kulin Nation. Affirm Press pays respect to their Elders past and present.

New York Amsterdam/Antwerp London Toronto Sydney/Melbourne New Delhi
Visit our website at www.simonandschuster.com.au

AFFIRM PRESS and design are trademarks of Affirm Press Pty Ltd, Inc., used under licence by Simon & Schuster, LLC.

10 9 8 7 6 5 4 3 2 1

© Alexis Fernandez-Preiksa 2021

All rights reserved. No part of this publication may be reproduced, stored in a retrieval system, or transmitted in any form or by any means, electronic, mechanical, photocopying, recording or otherwise, without prior permission of the publisher.

The moral rights of the author have been asserted.

A catalogue record for this book is available from the National Library of Australia

9781761639913 (hardback)
9781922419798 (ebook)

Cover design by Steph Bishop-Hall
Cover image by ColorValley – stock.adobe.com
Typeset by Emily Thiang in 11/18 Garamond
Printed and bound in China by C&C Offset Printing Co. Ltd

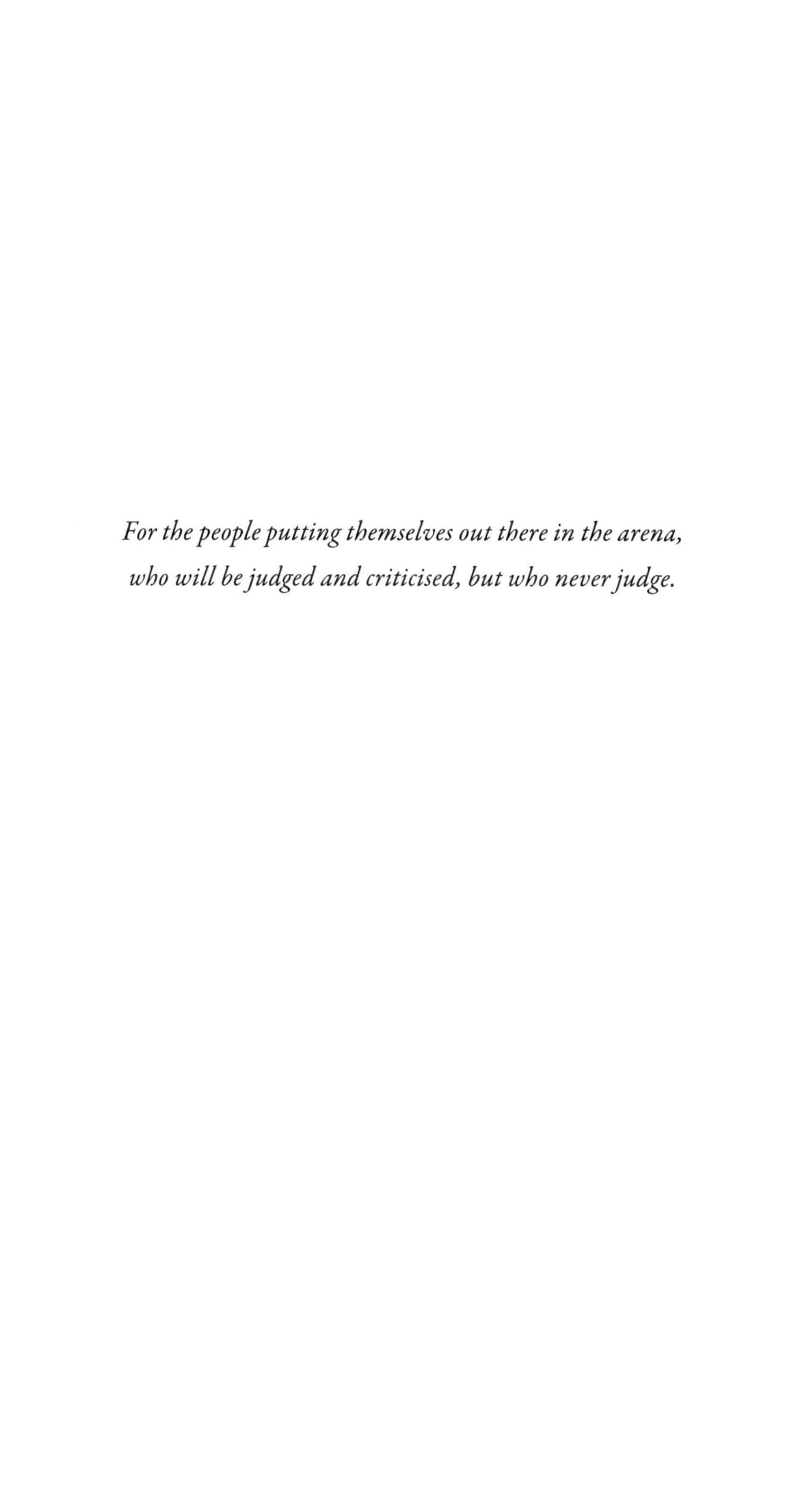

For the people putting themselves out there in the arena,
who will be judged and criticised, but who never judge.

CONTENTS

1. What does it mean to live boldly? 1
2. Your brain is either your enemy or your ally 9
3. Take a hard look at yourself 19
4. Attachment is the killer of growth 29
5. Your comfort zone is c*ck blocking you 35
6. Motivation – what's driving you? 47
7. Self-love vs self-pity 55
8. Set and smash your goals 61
9. Find your purpose 67
10. Consistency is key 75
11. Power routines to prep you for success 79
12. Hard action vs soft action 83
13. Maximise your focus for better productivity 91
14. Motivation to take action 101

15. The power of language and thoughts 109
16. Perfectionism 117
17. How does your environment affect you? 123
18. Streamline your life 129
19. Be gone, toxic thoughts! 135
20. Accept failure and setbacks 141
21. Move the eff on! 147
22. Embrace impermanence 155
23. How physical fitness affects your brain 163
24. Self-love hacks 169
25. Take ownership and responsibility so you can live your best life 175
26. Time to hit the ground running and take that leap 179
Acknowledgements 181

CHAPTER ONE:

WHAT DOES IT MEAN TO LIVE BOLDLY?

Challenge what you think you are capable of

Firstly, I'm thrilled you are here reading this book, ready to take the next crucial yet simple steps to transform your life. If we can achieve one thing together, it is to change your relationship with your mind and get you to become passionate about your brain.

We are going do this by tweaking and improving your mindset, thoughts, behaviours and reactions. You are going to see that by implementing some simple tools you can steer your life in the direction you have dreamed of. You will realise that people having the things they do is seldom due to luck or having things handed to them. Most people who have ever done something big or achieved something difficult have applied themselves consistently, with a disciplined mind.

This book is filled with tough love and hard truths, but it's only because I really believe that being honest with yourself and looking within is not just the best way, but the only way to permanently change your mindset and life for the better.

Live boldly

What does it mean to live boldly? It means taking what you think you know about yourself, the beliefs around what you have decided you are capable of, and recognising that these things are not set in stone.

It means being open to change, adapting to what life puts in front of you and making the most of every situation. It also means knowing that if you are the one who has created beliefs about yourself and your limitations, you are the one who can change and replace them.

So many aspects of our lives are due to decisions we have made, disguised as life 'happening' to us. We think that so much of our life situation and our capabilities are locked in and unchangeable, and too often that belief goes unchallenged. We like to bang on about how we are the victim of our circumstances, and that whatever doesn't go our way wasn't within our control.

We do this because this way, when things are bad, we don't have to take responsibility for them. But the downside is if you don't own the issue, you don't fix it, and so you keep telling yourself a story to put distance between yourself and authentic accountability.

The truth is that all these behaviours reflect decisions you have made at one point in your life: a decision about what you can achieve, how smart you are, how driven you are and much more. How many times have you seen someone achieve something you would like to achieve, and then thought to yourself, *Wow, I wish I was that motivated/smart/driven/capable/lucky*?

We all have a brain, we all have 24 hours in the day, and we all have SOME resources at our disposal. This book is going to show you how to maximise what you can do with your brain and your time. I will also give you tools to expand your current resources to achieve the life that you want to be living.

Once you understand that your mindset, thought patterns and the energy you emit are what differentiate those who chase and achieve vs those who live more passively, you will want to start implementing these major changes in your life asap. With consistency, persistence and a dose of discipline, your life can change in just a few months.

Identify mental blocks and be accountable

Now, we all have some idea of our true potential; however, whether you know this or not, you have drawn a line right through it in your mind. That line limits what you are capable of achieving – whether it's about physical goals, health or your ability to focus, retain information, attract the right people and be social and funny.

For each of those categories, and thousands more, you have let yourself know where the limit lies. My aim for this book is to challenge those limits. Now, some things may be set in stone (like your height) and other things that you have no interest in changing because they don't affect your life enough (like not being good at playing basketball). But there are also many things that *are* quite plastic/mouldable – things that you maybe haven't paused to consider before.

From now on, you are going to become hyper-aware of the narratives you tell yourself. We all have them, but some can be super restrictive and negative, while others are the reason we are resilient and able to push through any challenge.

This book is all about a no-bullsh*t approach. I want you to start thinking laterally and being aware of your beliefs around what you can and cannot do. Until you start implementing accountability in your life, you will always be in a place where things are not really in your control. I'm going to get you to dig deep and get real with yourself.

So you're going to have to trust me, because I sure as sh*t believe in you.

Chase the life you're dreaming of

Before you embark on this book, which for sure will be the catalyst for some change, I need you to make a commitment.

If you are here to pursue the life you are dreaming of, you are going to have to take a new approach to almost everything. That means NO procrastinating and no effing around. When I ask you to write things down or do something, it's not because I get a laugh out of it. It's because when you action something physically and in the moment, you instantly raise the likelihood of making it real in your mind and in your life.

You are physically making sh*t happen. So right here, right now: COMMIT. Commit to everything I ask you do to, no matter how simple or mundane it seems at the time. And my promise to you is that you will get out what you put in. I can guarantee that by implementing even half of what I ask you to do, you will see massive changes. So why not go all in and give yourself the very best shot at making that big, scary, brilliant thing a reality in your life?

Do we have a deal? Awesome. Let's do this.

CHAPTER TWO:

YOUR BRAIN IS EITHER YOUR ENEMY OR YOUR ALLY

A thought is a chemical

Let's break this down. I want you to gain an understanding of the brain and how it processes thoughts, senses and feelings. While this book is about mindset and thought patterns, we can't overlook the physical home of our personality: the brain. You can't have the mind without the brain.

I do appreciate that I am setting myself up for an impossible task by trying to explain the most complex things we humans have ever encountered, our own brains. I could be going down a deep, dark rabbit hole even trying. HOWEVER, I do want to give a brief overview of some concepts. I will only be scraping the surface, but I can't talk about the brain without going into a tiny bit of anatomy.

Our brains are an incredible network of neurons and glial cells, aka the supportive cells that surround neurons. We have around 85 billion neurons and up to ten times that number of glial cells (!!!). The neurons are the messenger cells, which receive, send and interpret information over nanoseconds, non-stop, across many different bodily functions – think everything from flinching when you hear a loud *bang*, to sweating during exercise to regulate your body temperature.

The collection of neurons and synapses that work together to fulfil a specific function is called a neural circuit.

Combinations of electrical impulses create 'action potentials' (the decision for a neuron to fire) and chemicals (or neurotransmitters, which are often described as our body's messengers). These cells form trillions of connections, called synapses. The glial cells are the supporting structure for the neurons. While we are still learning a lot about these guys, we do know that they provide nutrients to neurons, offer scaffolding support and clear waste and debris from the brain in order for it to function at its best.

Now, back to those chemical messengers called neurotransmitters. Each neurotransmitter plays different roles in the brain and they're responsible for every single one of our actions or thoughts. There are dozens of neurotransmitters, but these are the main ones for you to keep in mind:

- dopamine – the reward drug
- adrenaline – fight or flight
- oxytocin – the bonding chemical
- endorphin – the body's natural painkiller

You have all of these neurotransmitters in your brain, though they might each be present at different levels, which vary again from person to person. The levels of these chemical messengers are responsible for your happiness, the quality of your sleep, your focus, your attention span and how easily you become distracted, addicted or angry – and much more.

But the awesome thing here is that we have the ability to influence the levels of neurotransmitters through our behaviours, actions and thought patterns.

Cells that fire together wire together

The more a neural circuit (that combo of neurons and synapses that work together to perform functions) is activated in the brain, the stronger that circuit becomes. This applies to pathways that control movement, like when an athlete can perfect a motor task, but can also apply to the mind. Think memory athletes (yes, they're real!), writers, mathematicians etc.

You can see it within yourself: every skill you possess once seemed impossible at one point in your life, but they can become so easy you take them for granted – for example, walking, driving, speaking and reading.

The more you perform a task, the more energy the brain puts into strengthening that pathway. A strong pathway means less error, less effort and less struggle each time you go to do that task again. The brain likes efficiency, so it's quick to build on the pathways it thinks will be used a lot. It truly is like the saying, 'practice makes perfect'.

Just as this process allows you to learn a movement, a language or any skill, it's also how you develop and solidify your thoughts and beliefs. The brain isn't selective here; it will strengthen any path you give more attention to, and those belief systems are reinforced. Unfortunately, that goes for negative thought patterns too, such as anxiety, fear-based thinking, limiting beliefs and chronic stress.

Scary stuff, right? It doesn't have to be, and you're not a passive observer when it comes to the cognitive forces that shape your experience of the world. Just the opposite: if you're ready to take action, read on.

Rewire your thoughts and behaviours

Now for some great news. Just as the brain builds on networks and strengthens pathways that need more attention, blood, nutrition and energy supply, it can also determine the pathways that are no longer as active, and don't require those things.

You see, a strong highway is more expensive to run than a tiny laneway. Same goes for your brain. If the network is thick and strong, it needs more oxygen and more supportive cells that provide nutrients. So if the brain registers that some cells are not being used much anymore, it's going to strip them right back and prune unnecessary connections so it can redirect that energy to where you need it.

Now think about your thoughts and beliefs. Your thoughts and beliefs might feel unshakable because of how deeply they're tied to your culture or sense of identity, but no thought or belief is truly permanent. Similarly, a thought you might consider difficult to believe – for example: 'I am a strong and confident leader' – because you have always believed the opposite to be true, can and will change, with repetition and persistence.

It is literally physical change that is occurring in our brains via our thought patterns. Now you may be thinking, *You can't expect me to all of a sudden think happy thoughts and have all this belief in myself!* My answer to that is I don't expect you to, just like a weightlifter would never try to lift 100 kilograms over her head her first day at the gym. It's a process where, day by day, you become stronger and stronger until, all of a sudden, just like that weightlifter, you will achieve a feat you once thought impossible and be able to live with a motivated, healthy and focused mindset. Just remember, practice makes perfect.

Your thought patterns/beliefs determine your life experience

Now that we have established thoughts are a combination of chemicals and electrical impulses, we can say that a thought and the thinking process have a literal physical impact on us. It may be small, but grain by grain a thought can change our lives for better or worse.

From now on, I want you to look at your brain as your helper. Whatever you tell it to do, it does. We can't get upset at our minds for having spiralling thoughts when we have let them become an environment where this is acceptable, or 'what we know'. We need to debunk the idea that our brain is hurting us, or is the enemy or trying to sabotage us.

If you have ever engaged in these thoughts, make a pledge to your brain and mind right now that you will STOP using that language (even or *especially* in your internal monologue). Because believing that your brain is your enemy will make it so.

Decision time

Let's take this opportunity to turn your brain into your ally. Like a loyal assistant, it will eventually do what you ask of it. You just need to be patient, like a gardener nurturing his plants, so they eventually grow big and strong.

When you see small changes occur, celebrate those wins as signs of bigger things coming. Don't take them for granted, because if you can learn to appreciate the small changes and growth you have, that's where the great successes will come from. To go back to that gardener – imagine him celebrating when his first seedling sprouts a leaf.

He'd take courage from that early result and water and nurture the seedling until it grows into a tree. He would never rip it out and say, 'I didn't want a leaf! I wanted a tree!'

Patience and consistency will be your biggest assets when it comes to rewiring your brain to promote healthy self-talk and thought patterns.

CHAPTER THREE:

TAKE A HARD LOOK AT YOURSELF

Time to take an inventory of your own thoughts and actions

Hate to break it to you (well, I really don't hate it – calling people out is probs my favourite pastime) but for you to live your best life, slay and achieve all you want, you are going to need to do a purge of all the baggage and bullsh*t you are carrying in your own mind.

This is the most important step – why? Because without it, you will carry your toxic traits, limiting beliefs, and negative thought patterns with you into this next phase and stay stuck in the old version of you, when you are trying to be the 2.0 version. This is completely unacceptable, and we won't have this. Plus, you deserve better.

Call yourself out

You are going to have to learn how to call yourself out often and consistently. You want to critique your thought patterns and be the gatekeeper of your mind, carefully observing what you allow in to become subconscious thought patterns. Not everything can enter, and rubbish needs to stay out – rubbish that is fed to you by others, but also by yourself.

You are going to become really good at getting selective. First step: find out what your current go-to thought patterns are. Take a moment, grab a notebook and pen and let's begin. No, I'm being serious. Grab that notebook immediately. Do not pass go, do not collect 200 dollars.

Now, as you have probably realised, I'm going to make you work; life isn't a passive experience so this book shouldn't be either. If you can take action while you read it, this important information will be more likely to stick and become part of the new you.

For this section, I want you to write down all the current beliefs and ideas you have of yourself. I can guarantee you that some of these are not going to be obvious and you may even be surprised by how limiting your thoughts and the narrative you tell yourself, about yourself, are.

To get into a flow, let's break it down into categories. Feel free to add more to this list if that floats your boat.

- Romantic relationships
- Other relationships (family/friends/colleagues)
- Physical abilities
- Career

- Intelligence
- Personality/character traits
- Appearance

Now for each of these areas, write down as many things as you can think of that you believe or tell yourself. These may be positive, negative or neutral. But when you write them down, do so without judgement.

Don't avoid writing down a thought because you're embarrassed or ashamed of it; this is not a space for self-blame. By bringing thoughts – even the uncomfortable ones – into the light, we have the ability to destroy them or reinforce them, depending on whether they serve us. But if they stay hidden in the dark behind closed doors, they hold power over you. Change that today.

What do you want to change and why?

The next step here is to look at all the areas you want to change. For example, you may love the idea of being social with lots of friends, but you struggle to connect with people.

So the narrative you have told yourself = *I am bad at making new friends.*

You may really want to change your career and study something at uni, but you see how much time study requires, so you decide to stick to what you're currently doing.

Your narrative = *I am not motivated to study/I am not naturally smart/studying has always been a struggle for me.*

You may really want to start working on a passion project alongside your existing job, but you keep putting off launching it.

The narrative here = *I can't manage my time/I never have time for the things I really want to do/I am too tired after work to get anything else done/I can't sustain that much motivation day in and day out.*

No matter how ingrained a thought is, I still want you to write it down. As you do, you may see a bit of a pattern. It may be that you are not willing to try something new, because you fear failure or you worry about how other people perceive you.

For each of the negative sentences, see if you can determine *where* this idea came from. Did you always struggle in school? Were you bullied? Have you suffered from social anxiety? Have you always put others first, so the idea of starting something just for yourself is daunting? Write it all down.

And lastly, I want you to select the most important thing you want to change. If you had the opportunity to rewrite your life, what one thing would you tackle? What parts would have the greatest impact on the rest of your life? Repeat the exercise and come up with new ideas. Whatever comes to mind, know that I'm your personal cheerleader to help you make those changes. Yep, even those wild, larger-than-life ones.

If you think taking on all of those changes at once would be overwhelming, then start with the top few or even one thing that has the greatest impact on your life. Make that one thing your focus throughout this book. Don't feel you have to do everything at once. I'm not here to burn you out or add to your stress. You decide what works for you.

Now keep these narratives top of mind as you work though this book, because together we are going to rewrite them.

Notice your own BS

Now for the fun bit.

Well, 'fun' might not be the word you'd choose to describe getting real and shining a light on all the negative thoughts you've framed as truths in your life, but let's just think about where it'll get you. Time to call yourself out (YAY!).

Believe it or not, calling yourself out is a skill that, like any other, you will get very good at with practice. A skill that will get you in an action mindset – a position of feeling empowered and where things truly do start falling into place.

Why? Because this is the point of no return. Now is when you realise that when you rely on external changes to do something or be someone, you short-change yourself. Now is when you see that playing the victim only serves the old narrative that you have been replaying to yourself for longer than necessary.

When you push excuses out of the way, your only choice is to take action. Because making excuses or putting false limitations on yourself is the victim in you trying to leap out, be heard and feel significant. The more you shed light on them the less power those thoughts have.

Can't or won't?

I now want you to go over that list and ask yourself why things aren't changing now. Is it because you can't change them? Or is it because you won't?

For the items on your list you decide you actually can't change no matter what, just write 'can't' next to them. We will address these later in the book. Next to the items you COULD change write 'I won't'.

Now go over that list and say the 'I won'ts' out loud. Which ones are uncomfortable to say? Because you know deep down you *could* change it, but just won't, or haven't yet done what it takes.

Now you are going to rewrite that list, adding, 'I won't do ... because ...' and put the excuse you have used in the past to justify not doing something about it. Now read it and realise that your excuse only sounds good to you. No one else. Re-read it.

How does it sit with you and are you comfortable knowing that excuse is a reason for you not having what you want in life? Are you prepared to change the dialogue? Are you prepared not to seek to place blame on something or someone else?

Keep in mind this is not an opportunity to beat down on yourself for why you haven't done something. That is the victim in you wanting a voice. This is about calling a spade a spade, and getting real with your current situation and thought patterns that have gotten you to where you are today. Look at these thoughts analytically and don't attach too much emotion to them, because they are about to change anyway.

Sure, there may be some legitimate 'can'ts' in here. But I can assure you there will be a lot of 'won'ts' as well. And I am begging you to get real with yourself. No one needs to read this list but you. The biggest disservice you can do is lie to yourself at the very start of a transformational journey. In order to make some real change you need to be honest and straight up. And the moment you feel yourself lie, check yourself before you wreck yourself and go back and fix it. The time is now, and you are no longer going to put up with a BS victim mentality.

CHAPTER FOUR:

ATTACHMENT IS THE KILLER OF GROWTH

Stop being attached to outcomes and focus on the process.

Attachment is something that our mind uses as a protective mechanism. We become attached when we identify something as either good for us or as representing security or safety in some way. We then seek out more of the same in order to feel safe. BUT we often, and unnecessarily, take it to the next level by becoming attached to future outcomes.

We create an idea in our mind of what our reality should be, and we stick to it even though so many factors are beyond our control; for example: relationships, culture, aspects of our career and many external things that are in a state of flux. You see this in parents who raise children with an idea in their mind of how their kids will live their life – and this pressure to live up to your parents' expectations is where parental guilt and emotional blackmail stem from.

Having concrete preconceptions stops us from being alert and open to other realities and possibilities in our lives. That's why when I think of a goal that I want to achieve, I don't put too much focus on the HOW. I don't plan out my path too specifically because I don't want to get attached to the things I cannot control.

How many times have you not been able to have fun or enjoy yourself because you have spent too much time attached to the outcome, or expecting someone to do something for you or to be a certain person in your life? Then if that person falls short of the expectations you had in your plan it leads to resentment. See how toxic and unnecessary this can be? Not to mention a waste of time!

Problem-solvers and success-oriented people get really good at two key things: adaptability and resilience. It's essentially the ability to look at a situation for what it is, and understand that you have the tools to change your course and continue on vs the victim mentality, where you're not in control and when you see something not going the way you planned, you stay stuck in the past. Below are some common instances where people find themselves stuck, attached to an outcome that is actually just stalling them on their way to better things.

Stuck thinking the person who left you really was your soulmate and you will never recover.

Stuck thinking that job was really meant for you but got snatched away from you.

Stuck reminiscing on a friendship that ended and feeling you were wronged.

Stuck feeling that people owe you something, so the reason you never took that leap is because you didn't get what you deserved.

The list could go on forever. Having something unfair happen to you doesn't mean that it's okay to wallow in it forever. This is not to say it's your fault. On the contrary – if something *wasn't* your fault, that's all the more reason to move past it asap. If something wasn't your fault, why do you want to be a prisoner to those thoughts and feelings? But so many of us have it the other way around. We think, *Well, it was done to me – I was the victim, I was blindsided, I was attacked, I was deceived etc. etc. – so now due to that I will live a half-baked closed-off life.* ON WHAT PLANET does that mentality make sense?

The victim mindset is about as bad as resentment – feeling awful inside because you are annoyed at something someone else did. As the saying goes, 'Resentment is like drinking poison and expecting your enemy to die.' We ingest this toxic energy because someone did something bad to us, instead of sidestepping that low vibe, removing it from our lives and continuing on down a different, but likely better, route. Better because you are wiser and more resilient.

The less you attach yourself to how something *should have* been, the more adaptable you become. And adaptability is one of the keys to moving forward, growing and kicking goals. When you don't hold any resentment or attachment to specific outcomes, you can look at your course changing as an opportunity.

Live from a growth mindset

What does this even MEAN? When I talk about a growth mindset, I'm talking about the idea of accepting what is, and using what you already have to take further action. If you have your mind stuck on what should have been or what could have been, you block your ability to become problem-solvers and action-takers.

When we eliminate our attachment to situations and events, and how we think they should have been, we can accept the reality presented to us. We are more accepting of the now and more present to take action. This is being in a growth mindset: accepting that new things represent new opportunities and that closed doors represent other open doors, just elsewhere. Shift your focus, and lose unnecessary attachment.

If we think of anxiety as the gap between where you are and where you think you should be, let's work on shrinking it. Because if we stay in that space, we continue this vicious cycle of resistance. Learn to take the path of least resistance. That does not mean allowing sh*t to happen to you and not working or fighting, but it does mean learning to let go of what didn't come to pass or what isn't happening, and trying another avenue.

It does not mean giving up; it means exploring, trying a different route and using each experience as a teachable moment, even if it felt like a total failure at the time. That is what I mean about living from a growth mindset. That way, nothing is ever a total loss.

CHAPTER FIVE:

YOUR COMFORT ZONE IS C*CK BLOCKING YOU

Identify what is holding you back

When we think about our comfort zones, we think of what makes us feel protected, safe and secure. But I challenge you to look at it differently. What if you saw your comfort zone as everything you're afraid to lose?

Our comfort zone is just a collection of people, places, jobs, homes and life situations that we are afraid to lose – even if they aren't really what we want. It represents the safest option currently available. Not the best option, the safest. The one less likely to cause us pain or discomfort. That is your current comfort zone.

How many times have you thought about changing your job and the main reason you decided against it was because your current situation represents 'safety' or a smaller chance of pain or failure? Or how many times have you considered leaving an unhealthy friendship, but chose to stay because the thought of not finding new friends scared you? Have you thought about going on a solo trip to another country, but fear loneliness or the unknown?

Take stock of your current comfort zone. Some things you have here are actually the best option for you; you may be in a relationship with the love of your life, or in your dream job. Love this for you! That is fantastic. BUT I'm sure some things are not your best-case scenario.

Let's look at all those other things. Typically, you would not give them up unless you had a sure thing to leap over to. Again, grab that notebook and start listing all the things that in your life that represent protection from pain and discomfort, but don't make you feel empowered or happy. Then next to each item, write down what the best-case alternative would be if you knew you couldn't fail.

Why do we hold on to things that are bad for us?

The brain likes consistency, it likes the familiar and it likes to protect us. So often you will find yourself holding onto something that is not ideal or just straight-up toxic for you if the alternative is the unknown.

Take relationships, for example. People who love being in a relationship and hate the idea of being single are likely to stay in an unhealthy relationship because being single and not knowing what is out there feels threatening, scary and risky. So they stay in what they consider a safe zone.

It's that whole concept of 'better the devil you know'. We see this with jobs ALL the time. Unless you have a locked-in thing at another employer, you're unlikely to leave the job you hate, because the thought of being unemployed or working for yourself, not knowing when the next paycheque is coming in, can be extremely daunting.

Now, I'm not saying go quit your job. But it's a good example to show why people stay where they stay. Safety. Security. And although adventure seems inviting and super appealing, at the end of the day, for most people, security trumps adventure. Time and time again.

But what if I told you that you already have the resources to bridge that gap where fear currently lies? What if you knew you could leave that situation behind, because you *can* grow into something new? After reading this, you will have discovered that we all possess this ability; some people have just learned to access it earlier than others.

Staying in your comfort zone keeps you in a place of fear

The problem is that the less adventure we take, the more we lock ourselves into this place of 'security'. But the truth is NOTHING is ever 100% fail-proof. No job, no relationship, no friendship, no home is ever secure enough that nothing could ever go wrong.

We live in a constant state of flux, and so do all our relationships and life situations. Nothing is ever stagnant. And change will happen whether you initiate that change or whether you don't. If you live in a state of constantly wanting to protect what you do have, and fearing losing it, you are resisting the nature of life: change and evolution. You are resisting the inevitable, and at the same time you lose out on new experiences, new opportunities and new connections.

You could live such a safe life, trying to make the fewest-possible number of errors, and still find yourself in a situation where you get hurt – and having had a terribly boring time while doing so! The idea of a comfort zone is often quite false and misleading because the more we attach ourselves to needing safety, the more we focus on how fragile something in our life is. And because we fear losing it, we then engage in behaviours that are more protective and less adventurous, so we live smaller and smaller – actually INCREASING our chances of getting hurt.

Why? Because you cut yourself off from being resilient and driven by growth, you stay behind while the whole world moves on, and even the smallest setback will feel paralysing because you have cut yourself off from the flow of life and all these new experiences.

Time to jump

What would happen if you were to let go of your comfort zone? Could you fall? Yes. Of course! Could you encounter something you didn't expect? Yes. Could you regret leaving what you had behind? Maybe ... but it's not as likely as you think.

We anticipate regretting something when we feel fearful and protective of what we currently possess. We are so terrified of loss that we judge that even the smallest risk is not worth taking a leap of faith.

In addition to needing safety, we want to feel good about our decision to stay, so we demonise the alternative decision. We try and seek examples to confirm our decision, and often will find examples to confirm that we *should* feel fearful of leaving. Which then strengthens our attachment to our comfort zone. For example, stories like 'Deanna's friend Annie left her job and she was jobless for months!' might carry more weight than others, and we might selectively ignore the bits like, 'But she waited it out, worked on her connections and landed her dream job in a great new team'.

You will start to notice that if you live just outside your comfort zone, you are pushing yourself into new experiences constantly. You discover that even if your goals don't work out, you will grow, learn new things about yourself, meet new people and make some new memories. Eventually you reach a point where returning to what you thought you wanted would probably feel like a step back; you have outgrown your past self.

Tackle regret head on

Never fear regretting something; chances are you won't. Even if you fail. You will be a bigger, better and wiser version of yourself for it. And not to mention more resilient.

Usually the things people regret are the decisions and actions that they *didn't* take. If something seems like a good idea at the time, then it's not really something you can regret later. You followed your intuition and your heart. Your comfort zone is a big fat lie. If anything, it serves to strengthen your fear and reinforce self-doubt, but nothing more.

At the end of the day, the things that are for certain are the things that are within our control. Which is not much! And trying to deny that to yourself keeps you in a spiral of trying to protect what you do already have, and keeps your focus on that instead of expanding your mind to new opportunities.

Don't act from a place of fear

Being a crazy controlling girlfriend or boyfriend won't stop your partner from cheating, never trying anything new won't protect you from failure, being the best employee in the world won't protect you from losing your job.

Never taking a risk won't mean you will always be safe. It's important to understand that if we live this way, attached to so much fear and need for protection, we will never experience true growth that lives outside our comfort zone. By letting go of your need for control, you welcome in a different life.

The funny thing is it often takes losing something or failing at something to realise it isn't that bad; you will survive. In fact, you are stronger and more resilient than you gave yourself credit for. Why not give yourself that credit now and try and step out of that zone?

You are more prepared than you think.

The neurological benefits of trying something new

As I mentioned earlier, cells that fire together wire together, and the more attention and time you put into doing something, the more physical resources your brain will dedicate to strengthening those pathways.

You can influence the pathways and therefore the level of neurotransmitters needed in that brain area to create positive and lasting changes. Trying something new falls into this category. As you begin to throw yourself into new experiences, your brain is working hard to create these new connections – and it learns.

This encourages a growth mindset and while all this is happening, you are not using up energy to stay in a place of fear because your brain is too busy for that sh*t. You will literally start to separate yourself from your fear-based, protective mindset as you will be needing to put your attention and energy into your new projects, new relationships and new experiences. Sadly for your fear pathways, you now have way less time to fester and stew over the same sh*t.

Change what's possible

When you no longer have time for self-directed negativity, you start to change your belief system about what is possible for you. It shifts away from your conscious mind into the subconscious mind and becomes a truth.

You no longer need to be actively thinking you have a growth mindset. Getting out of your comfort zone and trying new things will switch you to believe that you are capable of doing things *even* if they don't go to plan. And when things fall apart, your brain is now more likely to switch into problem-solving mode instead of meltdown, retract mode.

Not to mention the health benefits to your brain! By engaging in new activities and forcing new connections in your brain you develop your 'cognitive reserve' and increase your brain's resilience to damage or degeneration.

The more you learn, the more you use your brain, the more you challenge your brain, and the more you engage with other people, the greater your cognitive reserve and the healthier your brain. It's amazing how taking action on things has real physical positive changes in your brain.

CHAPTER SIX:

MOTIVATION – WHAT'S DRIVING YOU?

Are you running toward or away from something?

When I talk about motivation, often people see it as slogging it out to get something done. Feeling that you need to have grit, hardcore self-control and this wild persistence to get something completed.

While this may be true some of the time, I feel it is important to break down my two versions of motivation, and how tremendously they differ. If you can shift which kind of motivation you are driven by, then achieving things will become enjoyable instead of painful.

Motivation to run away from something is something we have all experienced. It's wanting to lose those five kilos and hating the way we look, so we put ourselves through intense workouts, starve ourselves to get to a place away from where our body is 'acceptable'. It is cramming for an exam the night before because you have put off studying all term and now you have no choice but to get it done last minute. It is withholding from something you enjoy doing – for example, cutting out an entire food group or not letting yourself enjoy a drink when you are out – the crash diet concept. It is summoning all your willpower because the journey is not enjoyable and only the end result is.

Running toward something is the opposite. The entire journey is fulfilling because every step of the way is getting you closer to what is exciting or what matters. It's where even a small step in the journey can feel like an accomplishment. While it may take a lot of hard work, it is fulfilling and part of your lifestyle. It has become part of who you are. It is something that can always be built on, it is *measurable*, and it often benefits more than one area in your life.

Take losing weight as the example again. Instead of running away from the body and weight that you are unhappy with, try and pick a fitness goal where weight loss is a positive side effect.

Take running, for example. Now instead of losing weight, your goal is to run five km. You start with one, then you start to build up; now a positive cascade of events occurs. You are fitter so you sleep better, you can eat normal amounts of food without feeling the need to starve yourself, you see yourself improve daily so it keeps you happy, interested and motivated – and best of all you are feeling healthier and better.

Apply this example to studying. You find aspects of what you are studying that you are truly interested in. Aim to teach someone who knows nothing about the topic so you are more likely to want to learn, think about the end result of graduating and what that would get you. Start getting more interested in your life/work and stop perceiving it as a punishment, but as a privilege instead.

Changing your attitude toward what you are trying to achieve can be the difference between a short-lived crash diet or six-week challenge and a long, successful and healthy SUSTAINABLE lifestyle change.

Those people who consistently get sh*t done and seem to have all the time in the world, who don't struggle to slog it out – they have made this part of their habitual way of being, and living that way brings them joy. They don't have to withhold from things in life because they have found a healthy balance.

Fear vs love

So many times, we act out of fear and our decisions are driven out of that instead of love. This is disguised as being 'the safe option'. Just like living from your comfort zone, fear will do the same thing. When it comes to motivation, fear holds you down, and love propels you forward.

The main ways fear will crop up and hinder your motivation are fear of judgement, comparison and rejection, and fear of the unknown. It is hard to stay on task, heading in the direction of your goals, when you are being held back by these thoughts.

Now ask yourself the following questions to decide if your actions are more fear-based or love-based. Keep in mind that fear is more often disguised by something else, and we often project our fears and insecurities onto others.

Do you do any of the following?

- Not celebrate your friends' wins
- Judge people when they try and take a leap of faith and do something new
- Stop yourself from doing something out of fear of being judged
- Listen to negative comments and instantly take them on
- Feel that if someone else wins, it means that you lose

If you said yes to any of these (or all) it just means that a lot of your motivation has been rooted in fear. The good news is that you can change this, if you lean into why you do what you do and start celebrating other people's wins because it means that success is possible for you. Become a cheerleader for others when they go out on a limb, and that energy will return to you when it's your turn to do the scary thing.

You won't notice the judgement as much because you aren't doing the judging. You will receive support and make networks. You can switch from being someone who holds others back and feels held back by life circumstances to someone who lifts others around them and will always feel supported in return. Energy always comes back, and all that's needed is a few simple tweaks in how you interact with people.

Where is your focus?

Often if you try something new and get criticised or laughed at, you stop trying. You run away from the pain and discomfort of the criticism, and this stops you from going any further. But if you switch your focus from running away from the discomfort and from the negative people to running toward your passion, your why, and toward the people who see the benefit in what you are doing, then your motivation will change, and you will feel capable of sticking it out.

Most of the people who worked hard to get to where they are, the people that you may consider your inspirations or mentors, endured their fair share of criticism, shutdowns and rejection, but pushed past it to become who they are today. Everyone has their setbacks, but it's the people who have pushed past all of them who have got to the top of their game.

You decide if you will run away from the setbacks and hide or push through to the other side of your hurdles, your purpose. Every time you find yourself at a crossroads of criticism, embarrassment, failure and fear about the unknown, ask yourself: *Am I more motivated to run away from this or to run toward my purpose*?

Stay on track, and those who matter will be on that journey with you. Those who criticise will drop off eventually. They will get tired of seeing you live on purpose and will leave you alone eventually.

CHAPTER SEVEN:

SELF-LOVE VS SELF-PITY

Drawing healthy boundaries with how you treat yourself

Sometimes feeling sorry for ourselves can be quite therapeutic, but it can be a fine line between that and a downward spiral of self-pity. The problem with self-pity is that we stop looking for solutions, and even worse, we expect others to pick up the slack or give concessions or do things for us because we feel we have been wronged by someone or by the world.

Of course, you can acknowledge that something bad happened to you. But you can either sit in that or learn from it. You may not have any say over what has been done to you in the past, but you are 100% responsible for what happens next.

Unfortunately, no one is going to come and fix someone else's wrongdoing, so you would be waiting a long time. It might be unfair, but that doesn't change the situation. And sitting in the seat of the victim will only hurt you. It's like when you resent someone for something and that person may not even acknowledge what they have done. They are off living their best life while you are wallowing, festering and thinking of all the wrong they did, creating a poisonous environment for your thoughts. And you will find the longer you sit in this, the more you relate to people in the same headspace and the longer you stay in that bubble.

Learning to draw healthy boundaries for yourself

Don't make the mistake of confusing pity with self-love; it is the opposite. You are keeping yourself in a place of suffering. Pain is inevitable, but suffering is a choice. And so often we choose thoughts and behaviours that enhance our suffering.

Every time you pity yourself, you encourage yourself to stay where you are. You delay your progress and you delay your happiness. There is nothing wrong with being sad and feeling the feelings that you need to feel, but that is worlds away from winding yourself up with detrimental thoughts about what could have been said or done, or what should have happened. This spiralling is destructive behaviour disguised as self-care. Don't fool yourself into thinking it is therapeutic.

I want you to reflect on times that, through your own thoughts, you have encouraged that feeling of pity. Maybe someone broke up with you or cheated on you and completely blindsided you. Maybe you were betrayed by a friend, colleague or relative. You were unfairly dismissed from work or you had a totally unfair accident happen to you that impacted your life. Life is full of pleasant and unpleasant surprises and it is how we deal with these things that will determine the quality of the rest of your life moving forward.

Know where to improve, without criticism

Now, time for action. Write down times where you have slipped into a spiral and played the role of the victim. This is not about criticising yourself; remember it is just about bringing these situations to light so you can learn from them.

We feel pity and we spiral because, although painful, it serves as protection. We resonate deeply with our pain and it becomes part of our identity. To completely let go of that is not easy, as it makes us vulnerable again. It thrusts us back into the world where we could get hurt again, where we have to get up and try, and meet people and work toward something new.

Sometimes it even means starting again from scratch, which can be daunting. Our way of protecting ourselves is to stay in the pity cycle we know so well. It feels safe and from that position we cannot get hurt. But the price of staying there is too high to pay. Because you can't have both things at once. You have to sacrifice comfort and safety for growth. To experience the highs of growth or love or new experiences, you have to put yourself out there again and drop the shield.

Have your own back and move forward

This is where you want to own what has happened and the times you have been hurt and chose to look at them as times of growth in your life. Letting go of the resentment or grudge and turning it into what has made you the person you are today. You can look at these things and make a choice.

Has this event weakened me or made me more resilient? Has it lessened who I am as a person or has it become part of my journey?

Have I learned from this? Can this make me more empathetic and understanding toward others? Will this experience make me a better or worse friend or partner in the future? Always ask yourself questions to help you move forward in the most proactive and productive way.

This doesn't mean you won't be sad about what happened. You can still look back and it may trigger sadness; however, you can look at it in a fresh new way – as a necessary detour on the path to better things – and not let it be the cause of suffering.

CHAPTER EIGHT:

SET AND SMASH YOUR GOALS

Are your goals measurable?

Sometimes even the goals we set for ourselves are hard to achieve because we don't have a clear vision. So, how do you measure your goal? Is there a halfway milestone or other checkpoints? Or is your goal fairly vague – something like:

I want to get fit/lose weight/make more money/be successful.

If you are vague in your goal-setting, your results will be just as vague. Let's take a look at the goals you hold for yourself. You can break it down into different categories, such as the ones I set out earlier to explore your self-beliefs: romantic relationships, other relationships, physical abilities, career, intelligence, personality and appearance.

How do your goals fall into those categories? Write down goals for each category, then look at which ones are vague and which are specific. Now rewrite them. I don't care how outrageous your goals may appear to others. But make them measurable. Make sure for each goal there is a clear pathway, with measurable, practical steps toward achieving it, so you know the exact moment you have reached what you set out to do.

When I set myself a goal, I put actions into play, but I don't attach myself too much to the *how*. I am very specific with *what* I want, but I understand that my journey to get there can change many times over, especially as I get closer and closer to my goal. This is because as you get to your goal, you are going to encounter new concepts or people that may change the way you reach it. You learn along the way, then take those learnings on board.

Don't close yourself off to the opportunities around you just because you had an idea of how your goal was going to happen. Plan the action but don't get too attached. Stay open to help, to advice and new doors opening. You may get a better result than what you set out to achieve – so don't shut that out.

Work on big and small goals simultaneously

If you have a massive goal, you may think you need a full day to work on it or a full week, so you keep putting it off until you are able to give it hours and hours of undivided attention. But the truth is that life is happening and changing all around you constantly. You can't press pause, you can't rewind.

If you don't find a way to include working on that goal in your daily life, chances are you won't ever get to it. And if you can't find a way to make that new goal part of your lifestyle and a permanent fixture in your life, even if you do start it, chances are you won't be consistent enough to see it manifest into its fullest potential.

Hate to be blunt, but you set the standard that determines what you will achieve in your life. You can probably mention many goals that you have had in mind, but for years you haven't taken action. You were too busy, didn't have the resources or the money etc. But I bet you if change has been forced upon you – having to move homes, being let go from your job and having to find a new one etc. – somehow, in some way, you made it happen. You do have the capabilities to do these things. It is just a matter of how important it is that it becomes part of your life *now*.

Now think about the pipedreams you have for yourself. The passion projects, the long-term goals. Do you want to work for yourself? Learn a new language? Learn to play an instrument? Write a book? Travel the world? Move cities? Launch a product? What is your big goal or dream that you have for yourself?

Anyone who has ever done any of the above has not only set aside time for it, but has been consistent about it. Even if the task is huge and takes hours and hours to do, it can always be broken down into smaller pieces, which can be scheduled into your week. If you say you don't have time, then you must make the time.

Remember, if you want it badly enough you make the time. If you don't, you make excuses. And I know for a fact you *do* want it, otherwise you wouldn't be reading this book. You chose this for yourself because it is a push to do something that deep down you know you are capable of.

Start putting a minimum of three hours per week toward this goal. Some people can do five, some ten and some more. That is your choice. But consistency starts today. Stop prioritising urgency over importance when you look at your to-do list, because if you only work on the urgent things in life, you will never get to what is truly important to you.

CHAPTER NINE:

FIND YOUR PURPOSE

The importance of purpose

I like to see the word 'purpose' as your 'why'. Why is it that you do the things you do? And why are they important?

Understand that a purpose includes the effect you have on others. It could be your effect on other people, your effect on animals or even on nature. But connection with our community is ingrained in everything we do. So, whether your purpose is linked to three people or three million people, it still carries the same importance.

I'm going to get a bit deep here, but one of the best ways of finding your purpose is listen to how people speak about others once they have passed away. Often, they speak about how that person lived their life, and what impression they left behind. Did they make everyone laugh? Did they make everyone feel important? Were they the one people would turn to for advice? Did they start something special? Who did they impact? These are all questions that you can ask yourself and see what resonates the most with you. How would you want to be spoken about? That's a good starting place when it comes to finding your purpose.

Start small

You will notice that it is your effect on others that embodies your purpose. No matter how many people it is – what is something you bring to the world? Once you find your purpose, things turn from being a struggle to being a journey; the way you look at the things you do changes because there is a deeper meaning behind it.

Imagine if every morning you set an intention that you would make people feel better than they did before they spoke to you. How would this look? You could:

- make three people laugh
- do two things to help nature
- perform an act of service for someone you love
- make someone else's job easier
- and much more

By setting that intention at the start of the day, your day now has a stronger sense of purpose and the way you interact with people will be different. You will connect on a different level and your experiences with others will be richer.

How to link your goals and your purpose

Your purpose does not have to change the world, but it helps if your purpose has a goal to make some change. It could be something to change the world, or it could be something simpler. What if your purpose was to live so in the moment that others are calmer and inspired when they are around you?

Your purpose must be fulfilling for you, first and foremost. Don't be a martyr. That sh*t is draining, and you will burn out. *You* have to get something out of it too; you aren't a walking charity. Even if your purpose is to help others, it *must* serve you in some way; it must energise you and make you feel empowered.

You can't pour from an empty cup; I cannot stress this enough. This purpose is something that lights a fire in you that you can then pass on to others. It's no good to say, 'Well, I'm really good at being a nurse and I know I'm helping people ... but I don't *love* it.' That is not your purpose, even if you are helping people.

Purpose check-in

Write down all the times you have felt really fulfilled. These times can be random and don't have to be related to your work. Have you been really funny, and you enjoyed the effect your humour had on others? Have you ever been told that you are the best friend to have in a crisis because of your calming energy? Are you really good under pressure and have you thrived getting things done when no one else could?

Try your best to pinpoint the times where you felt that what you did added some sort of value to a situation or other person while making you feel great at the same time. THAT is the feeling you want to feel when you are following your purpose. If you can pinpoint those times that you felt that feeling then you will start getting closer to what it is that drives YOU.

I remember always reading those quotes that said, 'If you do something with passion, you never have to work a day in your life,' and thinking, well ... that's BS. I like teaching fitness classes, but I don't feel like doing this all the time. It definitely still feels like work! I truly didn't understand it or believe it. Even though I loved teaching and connecting with my clients, I was always pulled to return to university. I missed learning about the brain. I missed being able to dive deep into a topic that I was so enthralled with.

I didn't really know exactly what I would do with it career-wise, but I made the call and went back to study. That's when it made sense. I started following something that was truly my passion. I was so passionate about it that I wanted to share the knowledge I had with anyone who wanted to listen. And because people saw how real my love for the brain was, I was able to connect with them and tap into my purpose – which is getting people to change their relationships with themselves and their brains.

Find your people

This is a world of connection. How we relate to other people, and the relationships we maintain, will determine the quality of our lives. You can't get by in life without human connection. That's unnatural and not how the world works.

Once I found a way to tap into what my purpose was, everything really did start to fall into place. If you can authentically follow your passion, the people that resonate with you will find you, the connections will occur. People respond very well to other people who are real and passionate. Although I loved my job as a trainer so much, I realised that my purpose was beyond that.

Now I understand that quote from before, because my 'work' blends in so seamlessly with my passion and purpose that I would do it even if I wasn't getting paid.

CHAPTER TEN:

CONSISTENCY IS KEY

The brain likes repetition

Like I explained earlier, the thicker the neural pathway, the faster the information travels and the less effort it is for us. By getting into habits and routines, we allow our subconscious mind to take on that workload so that the conscious mind is then able to put the work of decision making, critical thinking and planning into something else.

Think of it this way: your brain has a threshold, a limit on how much efficient decision-making you can do each day. And as you start using up that quota, the brain gets less and less efficient and takes longer to make a decision. Something that could be relatively easy to decide may have you going back and forth between the options, struggling to settle on one thing.

When you get a decent sleep, your brain has the chance to recover again, and the next day it starts again. That is why we always feel the most efficient in the morning vs at 3pm, when holding your focus on something for hours on end is near impossible as that focus begins to dwindle and fade.

Now that you know this information, you can do something about it. ROUTINES! The more routines and habits you can implement to streamline your day, and your decision-making, the less you eat into your daily quota of decision-making. It's something you no longer have to think about, you don't stew over it; it is done. The brain likes this, because it feels comfortable and is more likely to use its energy on novel or difficult tasks.

How to change hard-wired patterns

You have to get really good at identifying the patterns and thoughts you want to change. You have already done the first part, and that is writing down all your limiting beliefs.

You have taken them out of your subconscious mind and brought them into the light. The first step to rewiring is to acknowledge. Because you have identified it as a limiting or toxic thought, the next time you think it, instead of going with that thought you are able to pause and remember that it is part of your list. Just doing this alone stops the downward spiral. Then in that moment think of two counter arguments to that thought.

Honestly, it will feel clunky and weird at the start. You may not believe the counter arguments initially, but that doesn't matter. The act of stopping that thought alone is enough to start weakening that pathway. You are stopping the repetitive thought and that is a HUGE step.

Before you think it's not possible, think about how you can retrain a movement pattern. How an athlete can retrain how they execute a movement. How you have to retrain the muscles in your mouth when you learn to speak a new language – this is all neural pathways and a thought is no different. Just like movement, it just takes a bit of time and practice.

CHAPTER ELEVEN:

POWER ROUTINES TO PREP YOU FOR SUCCESS

Now that you understand that the brain likes routine, maximise it. In order to get more efficient, let's come up with some power routines to prep you for success.

How consistent is your morning routine? Or you bathroom/shower routine? Do you do all your cleaning in one day? Or do you break it up into different chores for different days? Do you prep food or at least know what you will be cooking for the week ahead? Or are you like I used to be – where none of these things have a set routine?

Not only did I *not* plan ahead, I would stress about having to find a time to slot everything in and get it done. If something is scheduled in, and there is a precise way of doing it every time, then you never have to think about it and you save yourself time and stress. You already do it in some areas of your life and probably don't even notice because it's such a positive habit.

It seems mundane and so basic that we often leave these things until later, but it is all the little things added together that prep your brain to stay focused and able to dedicate itself to the important things.

Write down a list of the things in your life that you often leave to the last minute or don't schedule in. Or maybe things that you stress about getting around to doing. Write them all down in your notebook. Then decide if it is a daily task, or a weekly task. If it is weekly, schedule all the weekly tasks spread out over the week – don't make the mistake of bunching it all on your day off as you will start to dread your rest day. For the daily tasks, how can you make them more efficient and automated?

For me, my mornings are done in a set order, I cut out all the rushing back and forth, it's almost like clockwork. I even set out my outfit the night before. When you have a morning routine in place, the likelihood of you getting up on the first alarm goes up because it is now an ingrained part of your morning ritual.

CHAPTER TWELVE:

HARD ACTION VS SOFT ACTION

How to really be proactive

When working on goals, whether part of your job, life admin or even a university assessment, the task can almost always be broken down into soft and hard actions. It is so important to know the difference between the two. Often, we will take part in so much soft action and fool ourselves that we are doing enough toward our goals that we keep putting off the hard action stuff.

So, what the hell am I referring to? Let me give you an example. Imagine you are wanting to get into fitness. You really want to make it a big part of your life, but you have never done any sort of exercise, so you are starting from zero. *Soft* actions toward this goal would be:

- Googling different gyms
- purchasing active wear
- putting together a vision board of things you would like to achieve
- watching different YouTube videos
- reading books about how to put together your own gym program

ALL of these things are great, and important to do; however, none of them includes you getting too far out of your comfort zone. You are still just testing the waters here. And this is where a lot of people get stuck: in the soft action arena.

It's motivating enough to keep yourself going but safe enough that you aren't afraid to fail. It's a bit of a risk zone for procrastinators, because you are fooled into thinking you are doing work that will get you to your goal, when in reality not much is happening.

Hard actions would include:

- physically going into a gym and asking for a tour
- securing a personal trainer
- going into your first class or gym session
- setting an alarm for 6am to get up and go to the gym (and actually getting up and going!)

While these hard actions don't instantly make you fit, or mean you have achieved your goals, they are much more intense and focused, and I guarantee they're your best ticket to change and progress.

Strike a balance

Don't worry though; I'm a big advocate for both soft and hard action. And a balance of both is better than just all hard action. It allows you to plan, get motivated and stay focused, while still taking necessary steps. But the way I look at it, is for every two soft actions, I need to be taking a hard action.

Let's take finding a job. You can spend countless hours on soft-action tasks, such as:

- researching the perfect job
- looking at all the available jobs around
- looking into what that job entails
- putting your CV together
- sharpening up any online profiles you have

But the hard actions are:

- sending the email
- calling the contact
- going to interviews

It's essentially putting yourself out there where there is a possibility of getting rejected, but also the possibility to progress to the next step.

Let's break it down

Now for a fun task to get you in the zone. I want you to think of something you want to achieve. It can be a long- or short-term goal. And write down ALL the possible actions you need to take (you can get as specific as you like) from the smallest to the biggest. Then write down next to each task either an 'S' for soft or an 'H' for hard.

Now break it down for the week ahead: how many soft tasks will you do and how many hard? You want to be doing at LEAST two hard tasks per week. This is often what sets apart the people that make sh*t happen and the ones who don't.

It's easy to fall into this trap of feeling like you are doing tasks toward your goal, or talking about it so much, but when you analyse the categories that you are working on you often see where you could change your actions.

Tackle obstacles head on

I want you to reconsider what you think 'failure' is. If you try for something and get rejected, if you worked hard for something and you just didn't succeed, or if you competed in something and didn't win, or if your relationships have all ended badly, you may consider all these things to be failures. But when we look at something as a failure, we tend to discard a lot of good that was there too. It's the type of thinking that gave rise to the phrase 'throwing the baby out with the bathwater'.

You think, *Let's not do that again*, or *I'm not going to put myself out there and be vulnerable again*, or *I'm going to stop trying for that as I'm too embarrassed to go for it again*. From now on, eliminate the word 'fail' from your vocabulary and just look at setbacks as just obstacles, or a reroute. When something like this happens to me, sometimes I have a mini meltdown, but the next thing I do is look at the situation coldly.

Ask yourself this every time you feel you have had a setback:

- Do I still truly want this for me?
- What did I learn from this experience?
- What did I just learn about myself because of this?

- What was something good that came out of this experience?
- I like how I handled ...

You will find yourself become a whole lot less attached to the outcome and realise that often the experience or the journey could have taught you more than a win ever could. If you always got everything and were never faced with adversity, would you be as resilient? Would you have as much growth? Would you have discovered new paths or opportunities for yourself? No.

For me, when I look back at the hardest times, I realised they were ALL necessary to get me to reach the highs and the best times of my life. Nothing prepares you for life more than setbacks. NOTHING. Next time you have a setback, instead of beating down on yourself, just pause and have a moment of curiosity – what will this teach me and how will this lesson serve my future self? I can guarantee that you can get something out of it in the future. Instead of resisting, become acquainted with your 'failures' and see obstacles as necessary components of your journey.

CHAPTER THIRTEEN:

MAXIMISE YOUR FOCUS FOR BETTER PRODUCTIVITY

Your brain is like a muscle – it can be trained

When it comes to increasing focus, the number one best thing you can do is practise mindfulness. The impact of mindfulness on the brain's ability to focus is what an unlimited credit card is to a shopping spree. You won't know yourself and your productivity will skyrocket! BUT unfortunately when I tell this to people, the answers I get are:

- 'No, no, I've tried meditating and my mind goes crazy'
- 'I can't do it'
- 'I get bored really easily so that won't work for me'
- 'Every time I have tried to meditate I just start thinking of all the things I need to be doing'

The list of excuses really is endless.

The problem isn't that we are bored. It's actually the opposite. We are overstimulated. Our brains are overwhelmed. Most people don't even know how to be bored anymore. And the concept of boredom terrifies people because they cannot fathom being alone with their own minds, so they set up their lives to be constantly engaging in random tasks or stimuli as an avoidance mechanism.

This is why we struggle to get to the bottom of why we do what we do or why we are feeling the way we do. It's because we never really truly check in with ourselves. This only happens with stillness or, as some may perceive it, boredom. You have so much going on around you to stimulate yourself that you almost go into this numb autopilot mode, where nothing is exciting enough to stimulate you more than you already are or for more than a few minutes.

Distraction culture

How often do you find yourself watching a movie and being on your phone checking your notifications at the same time? Or having a conversation with someone while your phone messages keep going off, so your focus keeps switching? There is so much stimuli around us that we cannot keep up, and we then start to lose the ability to hold our focus on one task at a time. If the opposite were true, then the slightest things would cause you to be curious and interested, and make you pay attention. Instead, we're more distractible than ever.

How many times have you checked your emails, then your messages, then every single social app that could be receiving a new notification, only to go straight back to the first app again minutes later to see if anything new has occurred? It might feel like mindless messing around, but this is actually our reward pathways FIRING like crazy.

But where does it come from? WHY does our brain do this to us?

Ancient brains in a modern world

Reward pathways go back to old-school survival mechanisms. Let's break this down. Anything that is linked to our survival is supposed to feel good, so we do it again. Eating, drinking, sleeping, sex and human interaction. We need all these things to survive.

If you don't have human interaction, you don't have a community, a tribe, you then can't have a family and you can't procreate. So from early on we have associated human interaction with a feel-good emotion. When we participate in any of these actions, our reward circuit fires up. Neurotransmitters such as dopamine are released; we feel great, and that is the brain's way of telling us to repeat that behaviour, because we want to feel that feeling again.

Pretty clever mechanism, right? But the issue here is that the brain doesn't differentiate interaction in person with interaction online.

And it doesn't distinguish a real connection from a 'like' or an email. It just senses that you are getting attention, most likely positive attention, so the reward circuit lights up. There is a whole other cascade of events linked to this that then cause us to have an emotional dependency on social media and notifications, but these are the basic mechanisms that underlie why we feel so great and why we keep returning back to theses apps on autopilot.

The trap of intermittent reinforcement

Although we may not get an exciting notification every time we check our phones, or the person we want messaging us may not have responded, enough good is happening at random times, which causes us to keep checking every so often.

It's like a poker machine. Just when you may give up, you get a small win and that hooks you back in the game. We don't even need to win every time to be addicted. Just enough times to hold enough hope that it will happen again. Combine these two factors and it's no wonder your focus has gone down the drain.

Now try going from that headspace and then focusing on a task with no distractions for one hour. Good luck! You will probably feel your arm reach for your phone unconsciously twenty times in that hour. Or try to sit and meditate for fifteen minutes. Your mind will be going from problem to problem in your head, thinking of all the to-do lists etc. No wonder it's easy to just diagnose yourself as someone who can't focus, has an attention disorder, or is too jittery and can't sit still.

Time to unlearn

The hard truth is, that you, without meaning to, have set it up that way. Unless you have a clinical diagnosis, you probably don't have a disorder. You have just succumbed to your reward circuitry and given in to your cravings every time – so it's what you're used to.

You stay in an overstimulated loop that now nothing is truly exciting anymore, you just need that dose of connection or a notification to keep you at bay until the next one. Sitting still feels like an eternity and you feel uncomfortable in your own skin.

Well, as you know now, the mind is like a muscle and needs to be trained in order to perform at its best. Don't be disheartened if you can't sit and meditate. Now that you have a general understanding of the mechanisms behind your lack of focus, you will hopefully be a bit more patient with your brain – like you would when training your body.

You don't run a marathon the first time you try running, but you also don't get disheartened and say, 'I tried running once, but I couldn't run a marathon so I'm just not a runner, it's just not me.' You would be more patient and have another go. So why can't you grant your brain that same patience?

Hacks to intensify your focus and get more done

Meditation can be many things, but my aim is to get your mind in a calmer, unstimulated state. This can happen with a ten-minute focused meditation. You don't need to be sitting for an hour to reach enlightenment (although if you can get there then by all means, don't hold back). You can start with two minutes of mindfulness and build from there, and if total silence is too much to start with, either play calming music, the sound of rain or use a guided meditation to take you though. The health benefits are too many to count, and the more opportunities for mindfulness that you gift to yourself in a day the better your brain will perform. You will be sharper, you will get a lot more work done in a lot less time and you will feel more alert and energised and you are more present and not overstimulated.

Time block your day

Another great tool I have used for a while now is time blocking. If you are not already using this tool, brace yourself because this is a game changer. The brain likes reward right? So use that to your advantage. Instead of giving yourself the luxury of checking your phone whenever you want (it's actually the opposite of a luxury, it is more like a hostage situation for you) you allocate specific time to a task.

Take studying for example. You want to study for three hours. So you break it up into four forty-five-minute blocks. Set a timer on your phone, put the phone on the other side of the room and until that timer goes off there is nothing but study. After each block, you give yourself a fifteen- to twenty-minute break.

Your brain focuses a lot better in blocks because it sees them as achievable. Trying to hold focus for hours on end is completely unrealistic. It ends up backfiring, as we hold a half-assed focus, with our attention constantly getting pulled off task because we are fatigued, and when the focus drops we seek distractions from our task. This is extremely counterproductive. Four forty-five-minute blocks will be infinitely more productive than a 'whole day studying' because how much actual focused time are you getting in that whole day?

You choose the time blocks; it can be thirty minutes or twenty, but make it manageable and allow yourself the rest times to recharge. Now try to time block all your major tasks in the week, factoring for rest time as well. Once implemented properly, it will be one of the biggest game changers for your focus and productivity.

CHAPTER FOURTEEN:

MOTIVATION TO TAKE ACTION

Why the brain procrastinates

Procrastination is something that we all experience, to some extent. But for some of us it can be seriously detrimental and hinders our ability to action important tasks in our lives. This is sometimes considered laziness, but doesn't have to be, as it's also a way of avoiding something.

You may be doing a lot of work, and many tasks, but just putting off a certain job that is important, difficult or scary to do. It is an avoidance mechanism and a failure of your executive function. Here I'm going to break down some of the main reasons for procrastinating. Think about which category or categories you might fall under.

1. You are not getting instant gratification, so the task is not valuable to you at that time

If there is something else you would rather be doing (which is almost always the case, as we have unlimited entertainment options at our fingertips) then the likelihood of you doing that task is low. The issue here is that you know you are capable of the task, whether it's cleaning, chores or emails, but the importance or urgency is not there so you don't see it as valuable at that moment.

2. The discomfort of not doing this task isn't great enough, so you can afford not to do it

The position you are in now isn't bad enough that you need to get out of it. However, if there is something to lose you are more likely to value it. That is why you are more likely to go to a personal training session because there is more to lose. People see the value in paying more money as it makes them more accountable and it gets them to value the session more. A gym membership is cheaper and you have the ability to do it on your time, therefore you run the risk of putting it off for months before you set foot in the gym as you have a lot less to lose financially.

How can you implement this strategy in your life? If you cannot hold yourself accountable (like a trainer would) can you get a friend to help you? For example, I am not allowed to go out for drinks until my uni assessment is completed. Or if I don't do this task I have to put $20 aside every time.

3. You are scared that once you start, you will see how difficult/mundane/unexciting/time-consuming it is, so you'd rather dream about it than action it

Procrastination is, in a way, a flawed protective mechanism in which we seek what feels safest. And when we come across a feeling of uncertainty or the unknown, we tend to step away from that, so we are not confronted with the discomfort of not being able to do something. It is rooted in fear. And you may be thinking, *I'm not scared of doing the laundry! I just keep putting it off!* Well, you are avoiding discomfort, so if you have the option of watching TV vs doing laundry, you will choose the first. However, it's funny how laundry becomes a great option when you try and embark on really difficult essay. All of a sudden all the housework is getting done. Because in comparison that task is no longer daunting or uncomfortable. You will subconsciously, or consciously, seek a more comfortable option.

Get started

To combat procrastination, I use my tactic of delayed gratification – something my mother hammered into me for my entire childhood. I despised it but, lo and behold, as much as I (really) hate to admit, it's turned out to be super effective.

When it comes to getting to a task, especially starting a task, we often think we need to dedicate a prolonged period of time to it in order for it to be worth it. But the problem with this mentality is that we build it up in our heads as being harder, or more intense, we put the task on a pedestal. Knock it OFF that high horse immediately. Bring it back down to earth and normalise it.

Let's take writing an essay as an example. If you are one to start your essay only days before it is due, and then suffer from severe anxiety, lack of sleep and stress until you submit it right on time, then you are reinforcing in your head that writing an essay is an extremely unpleasant, difficult task. Look at last time! It almost caused you a mini meltdown.

So instead of tackling it differently the following time, your mind just remembers how unpleasant it was so it puts if off for as long as is humanly possible. So here is what I want you to do next time. Choose a time before you are about to do something you like.

Let's say there is a series you really want to watch, or you have planned a lunch or dinner with friends, or you have purchased a freshly baked croissant and *really* want to inhale it immediately (this is a big one for me) – PERFECT! This is the ideal time for some delayed gratification.

I want you to set aside twenty to thirty minutes MAXIMUM! Don't go longer than that the first time, because you will be less likely to get the job done. Then just tackle one aspect of the assessment. Maybe find two references, or start on the readings, or get well aquatinted with the assessment criteria.

The twenty minutes will fly by and you will have something to look forward to so you want to get it out of the way, and you don't dread it because it is such a short time frame. Now you are feeling less stressed about the task because you are more comfortable with it.

Bite-sized pieces

The more manageable and digestible the tasks are, the more likely you are to do them. The more monumental the task, the more excuses you can create in your mind as to why you will put it off. If you are feeling sluggish, or sleepy or are stressed or busy then you will find every possible reason to wait until you have a full day to dedicate to the task.

If you break it up and slot it in before something you really want to do, and you have to delay your gratification until after you have allocated a small amount of time, then you WILL get it done. And remember, because procrastination is rooted in fear, this tactic will help you remove that fear altogether. It makes whatever was daunting more familiar and easy to manage.

We have removed it from the pedestal, we have made it digestible. And when broken down this way, we don't fear it we just look at it as another daily task. The same goes for mundane tasks. Delayed gratification every step of the way. Don't check social media until you have done your morning routine, for example.

CHAPTER FIFTEEN:

THE POWER OF LANGUAGE AND THOUGHTS

If you say it or think it enough, the brain will believe it

The brain is an interconnected network of cells communicating via chemicals and electrical impulses, and because of this, a thought is also chemicals and impulses. Your thoughts influence your actions, which then influence your emotions and your mood.

So a change in your thoughts can lead to better feeling thoughts, and start a cascade of more feel-good neurotransmitters and hormones being released. As these go up, and as your stress hormone and neurotransmitter release goes down, you not only begin to feel better and more relaxed, but your focus and productivity also go up.

(Non-cringey) self-talk for success

We have all heard it before: affirmations, mantras and self-talk are key to success. On social media, we've all seen countless 'inspiring' statements designed to make us feel differently and to change our lives for the better.

I'll be honest with you, some of these mantras out there are so cringe it can turn off even the most positive people, and if anything, it motivates them to run in the other direction. And the concept of positive self-talk can sound pretty pathetic if you aren't doing it properly; however, understanding what you think of yourself and your abilities may give you insight into why you behave the way you do. A simple tweak in this narrative – the introduction of a different version of a story (or affirmation) – can begin to change your thoughts, and therefore your neurotransmitters and your overall state.

Debunk the nasty narrative

Call it what you want but there is a narrative that we have for ourselves and we have chosen that as our truth. Think back to the start of this book; I made you write down all the negative narratives you have about yourself.

Then you broke it down into I can't vs I won't. In this chapter, we are going to tackle the 'I won't'. These are the ones that can be flexible and moulded, because *you're* at the wheel – not fate or any external factors.

Before we begin, I'm not suggesting that you all of a sudden will start to believe something just because you say it. It can be incredibly frustrating when you have an ingrained negative self-belief or thought pattern and you've got these annoying but well-meaning people saying, 'Think positive thoughts!' Ugh! It almost strengthens your belief in the negative.

I understand it is hard to go from zero to one hundred with no momentum. So this is what you are going to do instead. Pull out the list that you created earlier on in this book: the list of 'I can't' vs 'I won't'. I want you to add any beliefs you have about yourself/physical appearance – basically any negative self-talk that crops up often in your head.

Next to each of these thoughts write down the best-possible thought you could have about that subject. For example, 'I can't study because I know I will fail' would then become, 'I can study anything because it's easy for me and I always get great marks'. Do that for each negative belief, no matter how stupid or ridiculous you feel making that statement.

Now, just like a scale, you are going to imagine that the negative thought sits at one end and the positive all the way down the other end. The goal here is to aim for neutral. Sometimes jumping to the extreme opposite feels so unavailable that it highlights how untrue it is and makes you feel worse. You can't often go from distressed to relaxed instantly; you can't go from depressed to overjoyed in a moment.

Often we need to find that middle moment of calm and peace. A neutral ground. Imagine if you saw someone crying hysterically, you wouldn't try to make them laugh; you would probably get them to take some deep breaths, calm down, have some water and only when they have released the tension would you then try and cheer them up. Because you understand it would be pointless to try to get them to an emotional place that is unachievable for them in that moment. In fact, it would likely make things worse. Start with that same approach to yourself.

It's fine to be just fine

Look at your list. Now for every statement that you rewrote, write the most neutral statement possible. What would be the statement you'd feel the least emotional resistance about?

For example, 'I always fail at every assessment' becomes, 'My past experiences with assessments do not determine my future experiences', or 'I have the ability to take action to change my results with my study'.

'I'm scared of dating because I always get my heart broken' becomes, 'Regardless of what happens in my next relationship I know I will be okay'.

Notice how these statements are not trying to make you feel the complete opposite of not seeming unrealistic from your existing thought? We are trying to neutralise how we are feeling. Once you can get to a place where you have less resistance to that thought, or to feeling good about something, then you can start taking it to the next step and be more actively positive.

Remember, it's a sliding scale. Don't expect to be able to feel comfortable going from one extreme to the other. Take it a step at a time. And also pay attention. Every time you feel uncomfortable saying something positive about yourself, ask yourself the following questions:

- Why am I feeling uncomfortable?
- What am I resisting?

- Why does this feel like an unrealistic statement?
- What is the most neutral statement I can make about this so I don't feel any strong emotion about it?

Unless you identify why you are feeling the way you do, you cannot get to the bottom of it. If you can shed light by answering these questions, you do it in a way that removes guilt, emotion and attachment. You can look at it as an isolated thought and not attach your sense of self to it, making it bigger than what it is. If you can get into this habit, you will start to re-write what you believe you are capable of being and achieving.

CHAPTER SIXTEEN:

PERFECTIONISM

Perfectionism will paralyse you

Perfectionism is a lie you tell yourself. It is an avoidance mechanism. It is fear, disguised as a need to work harder. Because we are scared of what people will think and say, we create this idea of 'perfectionism' to keep ourselves from exposing the raw, unfinished or unedited side of ourselves, whether it be the work we do or an aspect of ourselves.

The truth is, because we are constantly evolving, changing and growing, what is perfect one year you would have out-grown the next. So it's almost impossible to perceive your work to be perfect, as it is ever-evolving. When I look back at what I did one year ago I like to see where it wasn't perfect because I'm able to see how far I've come. I hope that in five years time I can look back at what I'm doing now and see how much I've improved.

This doesn't mean that you have to settle, or be unhappy with your work. You can actually be HAPPIER with your work knowing that it is out there, knowing that you have exposed yourself and your work and your progress rather than sitting on it and not showing anyone for fear of it not being perfect.

Perfectionism is fear at work

The times we are most likely to become perfectionists is when we fear showing our work. We fear criticism, failing, falling short of others' expectations and we fear not being good enough in the eyes of those around us. If we didn't fear any of those things at all it wouldn't remotely phase you if your work was imperfect.

But the truth is, that perfect or not, you would still fear these same things. Because everything is subjective. And no matter how good or bad your work is, there are always going to be lovers and haters of what you do. The sooner you get your head around that, the quicker you release your attachment to perfection.

Take a look at something that you feel you need to be perfect. And ask yourself the following questions:

- What am I avoiding by not completing this task?
- What am I missing out on if I wait for this to be perfect?
- What's the worst thing that could happen if it isn't perfect?

Often you may not know exactly what you are fearing or avoiding. By compartmentalising it, you are able to isolate it and see your fear for what it is. When you shed light on it, think of the worst case scenario, and then the most likely scenario, its importance diminishes. It stops having power over you and you are then able to take the power back.

However, if you keep it away in the darkness it will continue to control you and all your actions. Never avoid confronting your fears, that's what your ego and your protective mind wants you to do. It's easier to be scared of something the less you know about it. Expose those fears and watch them shrink.

What are you focusing on?

So many times I have felt like the work I'm putting out isn't up to par with other people's work, or I don't have as much experience or resources to make it as good and that then not only hinders my work but brings my creativity to a jarring halt. The issue is that I'm focusing on all the bad. All the possible wrongs.

It's easier than you realise to work yourself up about something. In a matter of hours you can focus on all the bad things about a person, a job, a location or a situation and be completely turned off. The mind is a very powerful tool and is very good at convincing you of almost anything. On top of this, the mind likes to think of 'like' thoughts. If you focus on one thing, it's easier to draw in similar thoughts.

Let's take someone you are in a relationship with as an example. Imagine they did something small to annoy you, and you sit with it, and begin to fester over not just this thing, but all the annoying things they have done lately, you then work yourself up to such a crazy extent that you are furious at them and your poor partner has no idea you feel this way.

Well, this happens with yourself as well. If you are working on a task, and you get into this downward spiral of criticism, how easy is it to then look back at your work and see only the bad? That's what happens with perfectionism.

It is an unrealistic and unhealthy view of your own work. The major issue with this is that if you stay in that mindset, not only will your work never be good enough, but you'll fear ever showing it to anyone else. You are so used to seeing only the bad that you presume others will feel the same way. This then stunts your growth and your ability to feel comfortable with what you do.

Next time you are working on something and you feel yourself slip into this negative pattern, intercept it with these four questions to get you into a healthier, more realistic mindset about your progress:

- What is unique about it?
- What about this is an improvement on what I have done before?
- What is the single best thing about it?
- What is something I wouldn't want to change about it?

Remember, the less you attach your sense of self to a thought, your work or someone's opinion, the less it affects your current state if it doesn't turn out how you expected.

CHAPTER SEVENTEEN:

HOW DOES YOUR ENVIRONMENT AFFECT YOU?

Your senses and the brain

Often when we think about feelings, we feel as if they are independent from the rest of us. And that we are at the mercy of our feelings whether they be stress, sadness, anxiety or better feeling thoughts too.

When we are weighed down by these emotions, it's not clear to us how everything around us is constantly influencing our feelings, determining if they will change or stay the same. Let's look at our five senses: sight, smell, touch (or physical feeling), hearing and taste.

Now we may not be responsible for what is going on around us but we can heavily influence what enters our mind via these senses and we have the power to alter them at any given time. Think about how music or a video can almost instantly change how you feel for the better and even for the worse.

Pay attention to your physical state

When you are feeling anxious, or stressed, your breathing is shallow, your posture is curved in or slumped and your head is held lower because you are in protective mode, so you start to physically close yourself off.

The interesting thing is that you can *induce* a feeling of stress or anxiety by taking on these physical attributes. But the same is true for the opposite. If you are feeling anxious or stressed, or flat or down, one of the best things to do is assume the physical stance of being relaxed, calm and happy.

You are opened and in a receptive mode. Straight posture, deeper breaths, head held higher, bigger movements, a stronger voice. This is one of the first things you should do in the morning: stand up tall, check in with your posture, take some deep breaths. Change your physical state from what it was in bed. Don't just crawl out of bed like a sloth, if you do, chances are you are going to feel like one too.

Implement positive circuit breakers

Time to get creative and start making some circuit breakers. This is hands down my favourite way to snap out of a low-vibe mood, or even an anxious pattern. It is like pressing the reset button when you need it, and the best thing about it is that it's fun to put together.

You are going to compile a list of things that can help switch your mood in an instant. These are then going to be turned into playlists, albums and notes. Break these down into the following categories:

- Songs
- Podcasts
- Videos and photos
- Memories

Now start to add to this list. Keep in mind that you only want things in this list that raise your mood. Songs that you love but make you sad, or memories that make you miss someone or are nostalgic, are not appropriate mood shifters and shouldn't be added to these lists.

Start compiling your music and video playlist and keep adding to it as you go. I also have a section of notes in my phone where I write down memories or funny events that have happened to me or people close to me, and I have this accessible at all times. This list just keeps getting longer and longer and it is now impossible for me to go through this list without laughing or feeling extremely happy.

It's good to have a few different kinds of mood shifters (like these options above) as some of these things may be better suited for different moods you may be in. Remember to make these lists when you are feeling good and motivated. Don't wait until you are feeling down or anxious as that will be the least motivating time to do it.

CHAPTER EIGHTEEN:

STREAMLINE YOUR LIFE

Identify the lemons

Something you need to get out of your head is that people are 'stuck in your life'. I don't care if they are family, a lifelong friend or a colleague. If someone is toxic you don't have to make time for them. Too bad, so sad, they forfeit the right to occupy your mental space. Start paying attention to how you feel after each encounter with people around you.

Make a clear distinction between the people who relax you, empower you or make you feel happy or calm vs the people who put you down, make you feel like you are never good enough or are always trying to compete with you. Identify these lemons in your life, and then manage your expectations around them.

Shape your life with love, not fear

Too often we stay friends with people because we are scared to be alone, or because there is history, or because we share the same friendship group and we don't want to make it awkward. But when you stop making space for toxic people in your life, you free up space for others. You start sending a clear message (to others but more importantly to yourself) that you have a standard to how you will be treated. And that standard does not waiver.

If you can't completely cut them out you can still change how you interact with them.

When someone lets you down or hurts you or puts you down once, it's painful. If they do it twice, it is frustrating and painful. If they do it three times, it's now just plain annoying and a waste of your time. This is where you need to learn to manage your expectations.

Snip snip (cut them out)

Stop expecting toxic people to respond to you the way a true friend would. If someone does not have the capacity to be a good friend to you, stop giving them the opportunity to disappoint you. These people can still be present in your life, but at arm's length. They are not the ones you go to for advice, help, comfort or to share great or sad news.

Once you start setting up clear boundaries in place toward these people, you will notice they will start to even leave you alone. When you stop returning or accepting their toxic energy, you are no longer useful to them so they take it elsewhere. If you don't contribute to the drama, the drama eventually dies.

You don't need to tell people you are cutting them out, or that you don't want to spend as much time with them. You can if you want but it's actually not necessary for most cases.

As you begin to grow and change people will either grow with you, resist against you (for a short amount of time until they get tired) or they drop off altogether.

If someone doesn't want to go on that journey with you or support you, you will notice this pretty quickly. You can put the ball in their court and, more likely than not, if they are toxic they will resist, talk about you to others and try and put you down.

This will continue until they get tired or find another target. It's a sad truth but it is also not your problem.

Don't make someone's issues your responsibility. There is a difference between being there for someone and being someone's punching bag. Never confuse the two.

A decluttered life makes a decluttered mind

Now let's look at your possessions. If you don't use it, if it doesn't make you calm or happy or doesn't have a practical use, then what purpose does it serve? If you have these items in your possession, they are taking up some part of your time and attention.

Whether you realise it or not: they are there, in the periphery.

Things that need to be organised or donated will take up space in your head, and until you get rid of them physically they will be there mentally. I like to use it as a metaphor for life. If I don't use something, I get rid of it. If something doesn't serve a valuable purpose in my life, I don't keep it. This should be your standard across the board when it comes to possessions, things you do, people in your life and everything in between. If your standards are high in one area in your life, they should be in every area as well. If they drop down in one area, then they are likely to drop in other areas.

CHAPTER NINETEEN:

BE GONE, TOXIC THOUGHTS!

Comparison and jealousy

I am going to go out on a limb and say that many of our negative and toxic thoughts come to us by way of comparison. Comparing our achievements, our abilities, our physical appearance, our past, our relationships and our possessions to those around us.

The problem with comparison, and keeping your energy out there instead of on you, is that you start to focus on what is bad in your life. You look at other people as the 'enemy' or your competition and this then causes a divide between you and those around you, but it also causes you to live smaller. The more you compare yourself, the more inadequate you feel about what you have to offer.

The hard thing is that often we compare ourselves to people we are closest to. Friends, colleagues, relatives etc. Comparison then becomes the root of resentment and jealousy and ends up being super damaging, not only to your relationships but also to your growth (honestly, what a buzzkill). Look at it like a sliding scale where comparison and jealousy sit on one end, and connection and growth are at the other end. Because if you want to stop feeling or acting a certain way, it's important to know what the opposite is so you can start to change your patterns.

Why do we feel jealous?

Jealousy and comparison occur when we feel threatened. The threat could be almost anything. You could feel threatened that they will beat you, get the job over you, get more attention, get the person you have a crush on, get more love, more money, more opportunities, more experiences and the list goes on.

We begin to fear all these things so our way of protecting ourselves is to distance ourselves from these threats. Our survival mechanism tells us that the further away we place ourselves from these people (physically or emotionally) the safer we will feel.

This is why you see people putting down those who threaten their sense of worth. Their aim is to get others to see that threatening person in a bad light, therefore creating more distance, and feeling more protected. However, this mindset is counterintuitive because it not only pits you against someone else (who could actually become a friend, ally or mentor) but it pits you against yourself.

Kill the need to compete with others

Instead of looking at others as competition, what would happen if you changed that feeling of jealousy into admiration? What could you learn? What could you embrace? How could you grow?

It's hard when our ego takes over and tries to keep us divided from those that we feel we are working against us. But let's see if we can change that narrative by starting to answer the following questions every time you encounter someone you feel threatened by:

- What do I admire about this person?
- If I could give them three compliments what would they be?
- If I could learn something or a skill from this person what would it be?

These questions are geared at getting you to see this threat as someone you admire, respect or look up to. You will be surprised at how quickly these feelings of fear, driven by your false self (your ego), fade away when you start to form a connection to that person. Not only do you get to push yourself out of your comfort zone, but you have the opportunity to form a connection and expand on your sense of self.

Often we don't realise how many things we like about someone or how much we have in common until we give them a chance. These questions that you answered will help you change how you see that person. When fear fades away it makes room for growth, friendships, connections and collaborations.

How do you perceive yourself?

Sometimes we keep our focus so outside of ourselves that we forget to realise what makes us unique and different in every relationship we are in. It's easy to be swept up in external things such as appearance, job titles and possessions when that is what you are comparing. And when you compare things that are not unique or out of your control you are bound to fall short at some point. So you then set yourself up to fail in your own eyes. This is where you need to shift what you focus on. Questions to ask yourself are:

- What's something I wouldn't ever want to change about my personality?
- What's something about my life I would never trade?
- What is unique about what I bring to my interactions with my friends and family?

If you aim to shift your focus to these questions and answers every time you feel threatened you will begin to curb your jealous thought patterns, come out of your comfort zone and increase your chances of making some amazing connections and growth.

CHAPTER TWENTY:

ACCEPT FAILURE AND SETBACKS

Can I regret this?

I honestly think that the word 'failure' is used too often to describe things that are not failures at all. Things not working out, when you come second or even last in something, don't secure a job, just miss out on something, your business doesn't do as well as you hoped or a relationship falls apart – all these things are often seen as failures, but what you think of as failure can change.

The beauty of changing is that you will start to perceive these things as lessons, or opportunities for change or growth, or even push yourself in a new direction. So many times in my life I have had incredible opportunities present themselves disguised as what I thought was 'failure' and had it not been for those 'fail' moments, I wouldn't have the skills, lessons, knowledge or have met the people I have in my life now.

Let's change what does and does not qualify as failure. Firstly ask yourself: 'Is this in my control?' I bet you try to take responsibility for things you have no control over in your life, for example: someone liking you, someone beating you at something or the feelings of someone you love. So a good way of testing if you really have control over the outcome is to ask yourself, 'Can I regret this?'

You will see pretty quickly that if you couldn't control the outcome, it's pretty hard to really regret it. Examples of this are:

You came third in a race.
You can't regret that; you ran your fastest and you can't control how the others performed.

You didn't land a role you auditioned for.
You can't regret a decision that a director made.

You were cheated on by someone.
You can't regret the actions of someone else.

You didn't get the job you worked so hard toward.
You can't regret what the employer decided.

As you ask yourself these questions, the responsibility and who had control becomes super clear. You also give yourself the chance to be more patient and accepting of the situation. Because the things you regret are where you made a decision, and often the things you regret the most are when you decided not to do something, not to try, not to take action.

Whenever I am questioning something that I need to do, my sister makes me do the 'death-bed' test. This is where you ask yourself: 'If I was on my death bed, would I regret not doing this?'

This has made me take action and try many things in my life. Because the regret of not trying something is real. It is a choice, and a missed opportunity. The regret of coming second is false; you had no control, you gave it what you could and you took that risk – that is not regret.

Use failure as a teacher

Now let's look at the things that you *can* control, and the things that you can regret. The times you didn't take action. The times you didn't see something through, were not consistent, didn't show up when you said you would, and didn't stick to a commitment you made.

For me, that's the only time I consider myself to have failed. But don't fret, there is something to be learned from here and progress that can be made. Failure doesn't have to be all that bad. You just need to be able to dissect it, learn from it and take those lessons with you next time.

Grab your notebook and pen and write down three times you consider yourself to have failed at something. But only write down the things you had control over like I mentioned before. It may be in your career, sport, relationships, starting a project or business, trying to lose weight or stick to a goal or hobby. Write them all down. Now see how many of them are due to not taking action, or giving up halfway/regressing and stopping before reaching your target. For these ones, I want you to write down answers to the following questions.

What was I scared of to make me stop?
(Hard work? Being judged? Not having the resources? Feeling alone?)

Would I still be scared of that in twelve months' time? Or was it a temporary fear?

Did I create my goal to run away from something or run toward something?

If I could do it again, what would I do differently?

What is the best lesson I learned from this attempt/ from not attempting?

What did I enjoy about that attempt?

Am I going to have another attempt at this?

If not, why not?

Compartmentalise the reasons, detach yourself from the outcome, find some lessons, think of the good, pinpoint the bad and decide if you will try again.

Remember, what you focus on will expand. If you sit there dwelling on the failure and how you may fail again, then it is likely that you will repeat that pattern. If you focus on the lesson and how you will approach it differently this time, you expand your chances of getting it done this time around. It is your choice, and your time, so choose wisely where you will be investing your time.

CHAPTER TWENTY-ONE:

MOVE THE EFF ON!

The past is the past, stop dwelling

Often we struggle to move on from something because we glorify the past to such a crazy extent that we feel that the good days are past us. This thinking is common after a relationship ends, after a trip ends, uni, school, a job or an era in your life that is over.

Now, not trying to go all negative on your ass, but you need to get real with yourself in order to get out of this thinking pattern. We have this twisted way of recalling things where we highlight the good and turn a blind eye to the bad. But have you noticed we only do this once it is finished or out of our lives? Why? Again, the age-old fear is back to haunt us. Fear is the reason this happens.

Think of a relationship, for example. When it breaks down how easy is it to think of all the good times (even if they were all in the first half of the relationship). We can have a thousand things we complain about when we are in a relationship, things that annoy us, things that we wish could be different. But then all of a sudden, these things miraculously disappear the moment you break up. The focus is shifted and we seem to forget, or suppress or even brush under the carpet all these things that were triggers for us in the past.

Rose-tinted glasses

Have you noticed that when you glorify the past, you are always talking about something that you no longer have? Either freedom, less stress or less responsibility?

This inability to fully embrace the now while staying stuck in the past will make you a slave to something that no longer exists – or only exists in your mind. Your current reality is influenced by what is going on IN your mind, so you literally are thinking up your current reality and playing it out how you choose to.

Sometimes we choose to make the past feel better because it takes away our responsibility to put in the hard work now to change our circumstances. We think, *It was just better back then.* Instead of thinking, *What big changes do I have the power to implement now? What action would I need to take to live the life I dream of?*

Often it feels too hard to achieve so we stay stuck in the past, reminiscing. And the funny thing is in the future, you will look back at where you currently are, and think of how good you had it now.

I can think of so many times in my life when I would glorify the past as the good days, but on second thought, with a bit of a reality check, I would realise that back then I was dreaming of a different life and there were things I didn't like about it, or was trying to change.

This is not to say you need to think of your past as bad. Not at all, but ideally you don't want to be perceiving it as the 'good days' because you are almost resigning yourself to that and the chances of you working to make each part of your life better than the last get slimmer and slimmer if you always live with your mind in the past.

Process pain and heartbreak and begin to heal

Now let's talk heartbreak. If you are mourning a memory or times you had with a person, remember that even if you stayed with that person, those times are still in the past. Attaching yourself to the past is not serving you and is a delusional way of thinking.

You are telling yourself that it was *that* good, all the time, and you know that is a lie. The reason you do this is because your fear-based pathways are telling you that you need a relationship (human connection) to survive. On top of that, you are having withdrawals from your feel good neurotransmitters and hormones, dopamine and oxytocin, and an increase in stress hormones such as cortisol.

Cortisol works by supporting your flight or fight response, and is meant for acute, short-lived stress (like running out of harm's way) so when we have prolonged exposure to stress and the associated stress hormones, it then causes anxiety, nausea and other stress related health side effects.

Due to these withdrawals your brain is trying desperately to get you to feel good again, so it wants you to go back to what you had even if you can't control it, or if you got dumped (I know ... pretty rogue of our minds to do this!). So one of the best mechanisms of the mind to get you to want to go back is by playing on your emotions: making you feel nostalgic, getting you to see the past through rose-coloured lenses.

It's a defence mechanism of sorts, telling you to return to safety, and trying to make your past look as appealing as possible so you don't have to suffer in this alternative.

Tell your brain enough is enough

The number one thing you need to do is to whack your brain into line every time it glorifies the past. A great tool is for every time your mind thinks of something you miss about that situation or person, think of at least two or three things that annoyed you, or that you hated about that person, and then think of one thing that you are grateful for since the relationship ended.

Here is an example:
I miss how we used to spend our Sunday nights.
Counter thoughts:

- *Wow, I didn't like that they could never be spontaneous*
- *It annoyed me that they were on the phone all the time during dinner*

Grateful for:
I'm grateful that since the breakup I've become so much closer with friends and have put some time into my passion projects.

There is always a sliver lining for every dark cloud, but sometimes you have to do some digging. This technique can end up being so effective that you can go from nostalgic and missing someone to laughing about how annoying they were and feeling like you dodged a bullet.

Even if you need to write a long, long list of all the things that were annoying, pathetic, a turn-off or frustrating about that person, go ahead. Keep this list handy as your ammunition and use it as often as you need to, to set your head straight every time it wanders down that rose-coloured path of the past, so you can start to even out those completely biased and unrealistic footage reels that your mind is playing on you. It's wanting you to be a weak dog so it doesn't have to do the work of healing after a breakup.

CHAPTER TWENTY-TWO:

EMBRACE IMPERMANENCE

Close chapters and move forward

I would say that almost everything in life is impermanent. Even relationships that last a lifetime go through transformation, as they are ever evolving. But the relationship that you start out with will not stay like that forever, and a successful partnership is one where both people can evolve without hindering – and instead supporting – each other's growth.

Even our wants, desires and needs are not permanent in life. But this is a good thing, because once you come to terms with this fact, and make peace with it, you are no longer hostage to this need for security.

Why do we put security before fulfilment?

Our need for security and permanence stems from (here we go again) fear. We think that in order to feel safe, the things around us have to be stable. But if you can create the stability within your own mind, not needing to attach yourself to external situations and not needing people to play a certain role in your life, then that is where true security comes from. True peace of mind can only ever come from within, no matter how calm or chaotic the outside is.

Pay attention to how many issues arise when we expect something to be a certain way, and it isn't. This is the root of anxiety, jealousy, possessiveness, controlling behaviour, feeling threatened, fear of loss, anger, resentment, nostalgia and overall stress. All these things get you in a state of fight or flight, feeling that you need to protect what you have at all costs, costing you dearly when it comes to your mental state.

Sometimes the hardest part of moving forward is closing the last chapter. If you have your heart in the past and your head in the future, you will never truly progress. You will always be missing someone or something or wishing your situation hadn't changed.

Hope is the killer of closure

I remember going through my first breakup ever. It took me embarrassingly long to get over that thing, to the extent that I would pretend I was over it because I was yet to meet someone that struggled to get over a breakup like I did, and I thought something was seriously wrong with me.

And I knew everyone around me was so over me sulking over it. But the truth was I still couldn't fathom life without my ex. Then, after a (very) long time, something changed in me. I realised that every time I felt the pang of anxiety or nostalgia, it was because I was hoping he would return or that somehow we would get back together. Then I'd feel so incredibly powerless about it.

The way I comforted myself was by thinking, *He'll come back*. This was extremely unhealthy for two reasons: I was banking my emotions and happiness on something that was totally out of my control and it was not letting me close a chapter that should have been closed a very long time ago.

The hope mentality kept me rooted in the past, and unable to be truly responsive to any potential new connection. Hope was stopping me from moving forward and letting go. It was a very painful way of comforting myself. I thought it was helping my recovery to hold on to hope, because as long as there's hope, you don't have to feel the full force of the blow.

But it was the opposite. I was telling myself I couldn't survive if he didn't come back, but of course I could! I was telling myself my life was on pause without him and that I was weak – when this was the strongest I had ever been.

I was telling myself a lie because I was scared of the unknown. The moment I realised this, and made a conscious decision to let go of hope, my recovery was incredibly fast and empowering. I was able to close that chapter and felt no need whatsoever for an answer. Killing hope was what I needed to provide closure for myself.

Allow for flexibility

There isn't just one way of getting where you want to be. If you can evolve to be open and accepting of new paths or opportunities, you will have the ability to move forward, happier than before.

There are so many different helpful ways of looking at situations. For example:

Things happen for me, not to me.

Everything happens for a reason.

There is a silver lining for every cloud.

Anything that can get you comfortable with the concept that change, expected or unexpected, will benefit you and your path.

Reframe your focus for a constructive path to your dreams

If you can turn your focus to seek out the best things that are happening for you right now, those are the avenues that will lead to new opportunities, new networks and new experiences. If you keep your focus on what should have been, or the idea that there is only one way to get to where you want to go, then you block out any good opportunities or chances that present themselves.

Take unrequited love, for example. You could be so in love with someone, hoping that one day they will love you back, imagining your life with them, having them in your daydreams and not picturing yourself being able to feel this way about anyone else because they are so perfect. What happens? You are at the mercy of someone else's emotions. Something you can't control. In the meantime, you block off any potential new connections with someone else, you aren't as open and receptive and you are almost playing a waiting game in your head – all by yourself.

What if you decide to focus on all the attributes you like about that person? But not that person as a whole? For example, you might love their humour, certain physical traits, their drive, what motivates them etc. You can learn to fall in love with that *kind* of person. Now what happens?

You are more alert and aware when this type of person comes into your life; you are open to new conversations and because your energy is different and more receptive, you are likely to come into contact with many people that possess these traits.

Manifest your dreams

This example can be applied to almost anything you are trying to bring into your life: a job, a home, a friendship group, an experience or a partner.

It's knowing what you want, but letting go of exactly *how* it comes to be. It's knowing how you want to feel and the experiences you want to have. You may get exactly what you want, but often, if you allow for flexibility, you call in something much better. Every time you bank on a certain result and become too attached to it, you end up acting from a place of fear.

This fear then causes resistance to what you are actually trying to get. We spend so much energy focusing on *not* having something that we hinder our progress toward what we actually want to have. We do this to ourselves, in our heads. And we can unblock ourselves just as easily. Focus on the feeling, not the physical aspect, and notice how the resistance you hold toward what you want drops away.

CHAPTER TWENTY-THREE:

HOW PHYSICAL FITNESS AFFECTS YOUR BRAIN

The neurotransmitters at play

Let's break down the main neurotransmitters/chemicals that are released during exercise, which in turn affect how we feel. While these guys are quite complex, I want to give a bit of an overview on what each one does, and the role they play in our brains.

Endorphins

Endorphins are a kind of neurotransmitter and hormone that contribute to pain relief and generally feeling well. Endorphins promote the release of dopamine and low levels of endorphins are associated with depression.

Dopamine

It makes you feel good, it's what fires when you are doing something that the brain wants you to repeat (anything fun or essential for survival like eating, drinking, sex etc.). This neurotransmitter plays a key role in reward, motivation and learning. It's also associated with addictive behaviours, so exercising can actually help regulate these pathways and is even recommended to treat substance-abuse disorders.

Serotonin

Exercise also boosts your levels of serotonin, which is a feel-good neurotransmitter but is also involved in sleep cycles, sleep regulation and appetite, and it boosts your overall mood. Consistent and regular exercise will help you get a more profound and solid sleep, which is one of the most essential things for overall brain health and function. This one cannot be overlooked!

Brain-derived neurotrophic factor (BDNF)

Try saying that ten times really fast! This protein, also known as a neurotrophin, is involved in neurogenesis (the forming of new neurons). It also promotes vascular (vein) health in the brain (better blood circulation, and therefore more oxygen to the brain for increased performance) and can even increase the volume of the hippocampus (the part of the brain where memories are stored). Endurance exercise and high-intensity exercise will increase your levels of BDNF.

How does it all work?

When we exercise, we wake up parts of the brain to become more active (parts that may be operating at a lower level when feeling depressed), which makes us become more alert and more productive, and because of the release of these chemicals, we feel happier, calmer and more focused.

How can we use fitness to alter our mood?

Movement comes in so many different forms. I am a huge advocate for regular physical exercise, weight training, running, walking, boxing, Pilates etc. and all of these are awesome for long-term health benefits in the brain.

If you incorporate activities like these consistently in your life, you're adding to your cognitive reserve and protecting your brain from degeneration and cognitive decline. Exercise also acts as a form of meditation, as you are investing that time in your body, learning new movements, and focusing on the task at hand and your breathing. This means exercise takes the focus away from stressful or depressing thoughts, and can be very calming.

However, a full-on weight session is not necessary to change your mood in an instant. Don't think that to feel better you need to commit to an hour-long intense sweat session. Yes, a more intense or longer workout is going to release more endorphins, but you can still enjoy the benefits from smaller-scale workouts if you are feeling flat in the moment and can't leave your desk to train.

I've outlined two ways to incorporate bursts of activity into your day-to-day routines. The more you make exercise a manageable part of your lifestyle, the more sustainable and helpful it will be to you, and your brain, in the long term.

Stretching

A simple three- to five-minute stretch will not only improve circulation in the body, and brain, but will also reduce mental stimulation, as your focus is purely on your movements. These stretches do not have to be advanced or difficult movements. Find a space the size of a yoga mat and get moving and wake up those muscles – however feels good for you.

HIIT (high-intensity interval training)

A bout of high-intensity exercise is amazing for a quick boost of feel-good neurotransmitters. You will get your heart racing and improve circulation, alertness and focus. All this can be done in literally four minutes. There are many different styles of HIIT, but the aim is to choose an exercise where you can hit a maximum intensity and have a short rest in between – think squat jumps, sprints, burpees etc. One example is Tabata, a style of HIIT where you go hard for twenty seconds, and rest for ten, repeated eight times for a total of four minutes.

Try incorporating these two exercise styles into your day – if possible, right at the start of your day to set the tone and get you feeling energised. The difference in your focus, attention span and stress levels will be incredibly noticeable after just a few days.

CHAPTER TWENTY-FOUR:

SELF-LOVE HACKS

Be your own team

My goal for this book is for you to commit to always improving the relationship with yourself. I want you to change how you speak to yourself when things get hard, or when you don't achieve exactly what you want. I want you to start to see yourself, your brain and your mind as a team. When one isn't performing, the other is there to support, like a real team would.

So often, people will struggle at something, or not do as well as they had hoped, but then because of this, proceed to beat down on themselves because of that. You wouldn't do that to your best friend, but sadly people are more than happy to be their harshest critic and to not be there for themselves, even when they need it the most.

If you can't be there for yourself, it leaves you relying on external factors for validation, such as needing other people, social media, your employment or your grades to make you feel worthy. You put your power in the hands of someone else when you possess that power all along.

A balanced life is the key

The things that will weaken your self-love include:

- unrealistic standards
- pressure
- cutting yourself off from enjoying things
- punishing yourself
- comparison
- jealously
- feeling inadequate
- negative narratives

This book may have covered these topics, but it is now your job to do the hard work, to take inventory of where these things are cropping up in your life – how they play out and how often. You have to shed light on them without judgment, without feeling sh*t about yourself.

This is a blame-free zone and the work you do around it is only to benefit your relationship with yourself. Every time you feel bad about yourself read back over those categories I just mentioned and identify which one is surfacing. Isolate it, and look into what triggered it or what caused it. Sweeping it under the rug will only make it grow into a demon.

Self-love questions to ask yourself

This following part is a really cool way of getting to not only know yourself but to start to grow a deep sense of respect for yourself. These questions can be done as often as you want and the answers don't always have to be the same. Take your time with them and think hard about each answer because there is always an answer.

When have I stood up for someone else?

When have I stood up for myself?

I was most proud of myself when I ...

My three most favourite personality attributes are ...

My three best attributes as a friend are ...

My three best physical attributes are ...

When there is a crisis I am really good at ...

When someone needs help, they can come to me because ...

I am really good at supporting people because I ...

Three things I would never change about myself are ...

Three things I would never change about my past are ...

The happiest I felt this week was ...

The three highlights of the past year for me were ...

The time I felt the most brave was ...

Something I have overcome that I felt I never would be able to do was ...

My most exciting achievement is ...

I want to be most remembered for ...

Answering these questions will start to get you to look at yourself the way your best friend or a loved one would see you. You can finally start to see yourself and respect yourself as you always should. Write these answers down and hold this list close to you and read it as often as you need. There will be times where you will need to feel empowered, strong, supported – and this is one of the ways that you will be able to provide all those things for yourself.

CHAPTER TWENTY-FIVE:

TAKE OWNERSHIP AND RESPONSIBILITY SO YOU CAN LIVE YOUR BEST LIFE

Act

As you near the end of this book, you can see how many different ways the mind can change your life for the better. Life isn't a passive experience. How you act and interact with what is happening around you will determine how much you can experience and what you can experience.

Control what you can

There may be so much in your life that you have absolutely no power over, but you can tell by now that there is so much within you that you *can* control. And if you can direct your mind to be your ally, if you can change the way you choose to look at things, if you have the ability to change the way you interact with people and learn to be less attached to the past, your life will literally change, and faster than you'd expect. But one thing is for sure: you need to take ownership of it.

Every time you blame a situation or a person for something you aren't happy with, you:

- resign yourself to be the victim of a scenario
- stop trying to change it, because your energy is spent on blaming

- stagnate your growth
- create a toxic environment for your thoughts

The hard reality is that in order to achieve that growth mindset, and all the amazing life experiences that come with it, you have to be willing to let your past self and your old ways die. You can't have both living side by side. Ownership and blame cannot co-exist. One pushes you into the future while the other one keeps you in the past.

Every time something happens to you, good or bad, it's an opportunity for growth and for learning. You are going to be met with many situations that give you a choice. A choice to grow and move forward, or to shrink and play it safe.

That is a choice, and only you can make that choice. The level of ownership over your actions will determine the quality of your life moving forward.

CHAPTER TWENTY-SIX:

TIME TO HIT THE GROUND RUNNING AND TAKE THAT LEAP

You made it! You have reached the end of this book, equipped now with a deeper understanding (and love!) for your brain and for yourself. Now is the time to grab everything you want to absorb from this book and take that leap. There is only so much thinking and planning that you need to do, but life is an active experience, so let's make it that.

Never be afraid to 'fail'. There is nothing wrong with falling short, or not getting where you wanted to. Setbacks are part of the journey, and not taking action and not trying is the only way you can truly fail at something. Criticisms should never be the reason you don't do something, because those who criticise you are not the reason you do what you do, so don't let them be the reason you stop. Pay attention to the role fear plays in your life. You choose how big its role in your life will be.

Every day can be a fresh start. Every day can be a reset. We all have twenty-four hours in a day; we all have the chance to be accountable and take consistent action every day. We all have the ability to work toward something, whether slow or fast. And we all have the choice to do something or to not.

How are you going to live your life, and what legacy do you want to leave behind? Instead of worrying about the past and things that may never happen, why not take a chance on the unknown?

If you release the need to be accepted by others, the need for people that you don't even know to like you etc. – that cleanse is the first step to greatness. If you can give less of a f*ck about the people that are irrelevant and more of a f*ck to the ones that matter, then you are on track to living your best, most adventure filled life ever.

Now that you know that your mind has the ability to be your biggest ally, make it so. You have an incredible power within your mind. A power to change how you experience life, how you grow and what you are feeling. You may not be able to control a lot of what goes on outside of you, but what you can control is pretty incredible: your mind. Don't take it for granted, don't live a passive life. Remember that life isn't happening to you, it is happening for you. Action will always get you further than inaction, so start now, flaws, speedbumps and all. It's all part of the journey.

And lastly, remember to be kind to yourself, be kind to your brain and don't take sh*t from anyone – especially not yourself. Big love.

ACKNOWLEDGEMENTS

I want to thank my entire family for teaching me what real love and relationships are.

Thank you to my best friends who have built me up and been my number one supporters through the many different stages of my life so far. To all my podcast listeners who have allowed me to have a voice and share my passion for the brain.

Thank you to my incredible editor, Freya, and my publisher, Affirm Press, for creating this opportunity, and somehow knowing that it has always been my dream to write a book.

And lastly, I am grateful for all the experiences in my life. The good, the bad and the ugly. For those are the lessons that have allowed me to be where I am today.

ALSO BY ALEXIS FERNANDEZ-PREIKSA ...

THE NEUROSCIENCE OF SELF-LOVE

Thoughts and moods are chemical reactions in your brain that you might think you are powerless to control. But modern science has shown beyond doubt that changing your behaviour and thought patterns can rewire the neurological pathways of your brain to literally change how you think, feel and view yourself.

In *The Neuroscience of Self-Love*, Alexis Fernandez-Preiksa takes the theory out of neuroscience and gives you practical tools and exercises to create a new self that is happier, more balanced and less dependent on others for validation. By re-engineering your habits, optimising your decision-making, curbing negative thoughts and harnessing the power of exercise and meditation, you will become more centred, connected and creative, and learn how to trust, prioritise and truly love yourself.

ALSO BY ALEXIS FERNANDEZ-PREIKSA …

HOW TO CHASE CHANGE

If you want to change your life, but you don't know where to start, know that you already possess your most powerful tool: your mind. *How to Chase Change* is the ultimate guide to utilising your mindset to become your best self. This 30-day program covers everything from turning aspirational goals into action, increasing self-confidence and overcoming heartbreak, to eliminating negative self-talk and committing to small changes that will help you achieve big results.

In *How to Chase Change*, neuroscientist and beloved podcast host Alexis Fernandez-Preiksa combines fascinating tidbits of research on the human brain, poignant inspirational moments, and insight from her own experiences to give you everything you need to create lasting, positive change. Each module is designed around timeless wisdom you can return to again and again as you work through different challenges and transitions.